Birds
in your
Garden

Nicholas Hammond
and Bruce Pearson

HAMLYN

First published in 1995 by Hamlyn Limited,
an imprint of Reed Consumer Books Limited
Michelin House, 81 Fulham Road, London SW3 6RB

Copyright © Reed International Books Limited 1995

Text copyright © Nicholas Hammond 1995
Illustrations copyright © Bruce Pearson 1995

The photographs are reproduced by pemission of the following:
Roger Tidman: pp. 6, 8–9, 10, 13, 17, 37, 42 (left), 46 (2), 47,
48, 55, 58, 59, 61, 62–3, 64–5, 78, 98–99, 101, 104, 107, 108,
112, 113, 120, 128, 132–3, 136–7
Roger Wilmshurst: pp 11, 16, 19, 22, 23, 26, 27, 36 (3),
42 (right), 65, 79, 87, 88, 89, 122–3,

ISBN   0 600 58249 3

All rights reserved. Apart from any fair dealing for the purpose
of private study, research, criticism or review, as permitted
under the Copyright Designs and Patents Act, 1988, no part of
this publication may be reproduced, stored in a retrieval system,
or transmitted in any form or by any means, electronic,
electrical, chemical, mechanical, optical, photocopying,
recording, or otherwise, without prior written permission.
All enquiries should be addressed to the Publishers.

A CIP catalogue record for this book is available
from the British Library

Executive Art Editor Vivienne Brar
Designer Richard Scott
Editors Samantha Ward-Dutton and Cathy Lowne
Assistant Editor Claire Musters

Printed in Hong Kong

CONTENTS

Introduction

Garden birds, unlike other groups of birds such as wildfowl, gulls or birds of prey, are defined by the type of place in which they are found rather than by their close relationship to similar species. Many different species can be described as 'garden birds' merely through the fact of they appear in gardens.

Which birds appear in each garden will be determined by where it is, how big it is and what is in it. For example, a large garden with mature trees in rural Wales is likely to attract buzzards, while black redstarts, which are rare in Britain, may be common visitors to urban gardens in Germany and robins, such familiar inhabitants of British gardens, are more likely to be seen in woodland in parts of continental Europe.

In most gardens the bulk of the birds are woodland species which have managed to find enough similarities between their natural habitat and the gardens that people have created. Houses, outbuildings, sheds and fences all have features which substitute for the nest-sites found in trees, caves and rock-faces, while garden plants provide food and shelter for birds.

Everything a garden bird does has its reason, although we may not be sure what that reason is. The purpose of this book is to explain what the birds in your garden and in the sky above it are doing and, where possible, why they are doing it.

There are five main sections. The first and longest covers feeding and the way in which birds manage to exploit every source of food. The next section explains the complex process of breeding, including territory, song, displays and rearing young. The third section is devoted to the development of birds and the importance of their feathers, a physical feature that makes them unique as a group of animals. Migration and movements of garden birds are the subject of the fourth section and, finally, the fifth section covers roosting and sleep, among the least observed aspects of bird behaviour.

This book aims to increase your enjoyment of your garden birds by helping you to understand what they are doing. And, by gaining an understanding of their needs, you can also create the right conditions which will encourage the greatest variety of birds.

Feeding

Finding, catching and eating food

Providing food for birds is the key to attracting them to your garden. If your garden supplies a wide variety of food, you will attract a greater variety of birds. A barren concrete garden will have very few, if any, birds. On the other hand a garden with plenty of cover and native plants, as well as a well-stocked bird-table, will have plenty to attract a variety of birds.

Finding food

In most cases a bird's bill shape will give you clues to what it eats and how it finds its food. Bills are used to pick food from the ground, tree trunks, branches, leaves or flowers and have, therefore, become adapted to deal with particular types of food. To pluck tiny insects from spruce needles the goldcrest must have a finely pointed bill like the finest of jewellers' tweezers, while the greenfinch, a specialist in the seeds, has heavy mandibles with which to crack open husks.

Birds of prey often catch animals too large to be swallowed in one mouthful. Instead the flesh has to be torn off in convenient bite-sized lumps and for this they need hooked bills with which they can tear through skin and sinew. Fish-eaters, like kingfishers and herons, may visit garden ponds in search of gold-fish. Having caught a fish, the bird must swallow it before it can slither back to the water. Despite the dif-ferences in size, the kingfisher and heron both have a dagger-shaped bill long enough to hold their prey securely before swallowing it head first.

In addition to having specially adapted bills, birds have other physical adaptations to their ways of finding food. Woodpeckers have feet that enable them to cling

Great spotted woodpecker on peanuts. The red head indicates that this is a young bird.

to upright tree trunks, while the feet of birds of prey enable them to grip struggling prey, while swallows have wings and tails that enable them to twist and turn rapidly in flight so they can catch insects on the wing.

In the rest of this chapter, we concentrate on five categories of food and how birds cope with them – seeds; berries, fruit and nuts; insects and other invertebrates; other birds and small mammals; and fish. However, few garden birds feed exclusively on one type of food. For example, seed-eating finches with families of young to feed will catch insects during the breeding season and insect-eating tits will eat small seeds in winter as their insect food becomes scarce.

Seed-eaters

Seeds are usually contained in hard husks, which a bird must crush before it can reach the kernel. The typical seed-eater has a heavy bill and powerful jaw muscles which make it capable of cracking the husk, after which the bird performs a delicate operation with its tongue to discard the inedible pieces.

Finches

A finch's bill is not just a pair of mandibles that fit neatly one on top of the other. The upper mandible is grooved, rather like the crown of a human molar, and when the bill is closed the top edge of the lower mandible fits neatly into the groove. The groove is widest near the base of the bill and narrowest at its tip and so that the larger the seed, the nearer it is held to the base of the bill. Using its tongue, the bird steadies a seed in the groove in its upper mandible and brings the lower mandible upwards to work between husk and kernel and with its tongue the bird turns the seed until the husk is peeled and discarded. This takes a few

Coping without teeth

Modern birds have evolved without teeth (teeth would add front-end weight and make flying less efficient). As birds use up energy quickly, they need to absorb food rapidly and frequently and, because they have no teeth, they have had to develop another method of chewing. The gizzard is surrounded by muscles and situated near the bird's centre of gravity. A bird will swallow grit and small stones and, with the muscles of the gizzard, grind the food which has been stored in its crop.

seconds and, while several seeds may be held in the bill at one time, each is dehusked in succession.

Shape is all

Although all finches have cone-shaped bills, the shape is slightly different between species, which enables each to eat different types of seed from the others and thus avoid competition. The more delicate the method of feeding, and the more deeply hidden the seeds, the longer and more pointed the finch's bill. While more pointed bills encourage more efficient probing, they do not have the crushing power of the heavier bills.

Goldfinches feed on seeds of teasels and thistles.

Goldfinches

A goldfinch's bill is long and narrow to probe for seeds buried deeply in the heads of thistles, burdocks and teasels. Although thistledown has a reputation for lightness and softness, when it is still on the plant it is packed very tightly, making the seeds difficult to reach. The goldfinch has particularly well-developed jaw muscles to prise apart the individual seed-heads.

The goldfinch also has other adaptations to help it get at these seeds. Probing teasel-heads is a prickly business and the red facial feathers of this colourful finch are short and stiff, which may help to protect its face. Being light and agile, goldfinches are able to balance on the swaying heads of plants when they are feeding, but they prefer to take seed-heads that have fallen to the ground. They feed in small flocks and may visit gardens to feed on herbaceous plants, especially daisies and other members of the Compositae family that have been allowed to go to seed.

When perched, a goldfinch can feed by bending forward to reach the seeds deep in the dried flowerhead of a teasel or by hanging beneath a thistle-head. To take the seeds of a weak-stemmed plant like the dandelion close to the ground, it perches halfway up the stem, using its weight to bend the plant to the ground, where it secures the seed-head under its foot.

Siskins

Extracting seeds from pine-cones as they start to open needs a tweezer-like bill and siskins, which are smaller than goldfinches, manage this quite well. However, they cannot open closed cones and so they must wait for them to open partially.

Another favourite foodstuff for siskins is alder seeds and in winter they feed in flocks with redpolls, hanging acrobatically from the tips of branches. Once the alder crop is exhausted, siskins move into gardens where they feed on the seeds of *Cupressus leylandii*, which are popular in gardens, and on seeds and peanuts at bird-tables.

Seeing red

Attract siskins by putting out peanuts in a red net bag. For some reason they find them hard to resist and will use them rather than other feeders.

Chaffinches

The ability to feed on a wide variety of food has made the chaffinch a very common bird across Europe. It eats the most varied range of food of all the finches – seeds of more than 100 plant species have been recorded in its diet. Outside the breeding season, chaffinches feed mainly on seeds and other plant material, but during the breeding season their main food is insects and other small animals such as spiders. Almost all of their seed food is picked delicately from the ground with their comparatively long bills.

Although only slightly longer than the goldfinch, the ground-feeding chaffinch is much heavier and, unlike most other finches, it can run as well as hop on the ground. This versatility allows it to cover different types of ground more quickly when feeding.

A redpoll on alder catkins.

The bullfinch's short, rounded bill is ideal for tearing into buds and berries. The 'keys' of the ash are a favourite food, but these birds will also turn to the buds of fruit trees, causing very unwelcome damage.

Preferred seeds

Experiments in feeding captive chaffinches showed that their order of preference for seeds was hemp, sunflower, grass, rape and linseed. On average they took 2.4 seconds to dehusk rape-seed and 41.4 seconds for sunflower.

Serins

A southern European species, the serin has spread north across Europe and has even bred occasionally in southern England. In southern Europe it is often found near human settlements, in gardens, orchards, vineyards and cemeteries. The smallest of European finches, it is rather dumpy and has a short, broad bill, which it uses to strip petals to reach seeds and to tear catkins to pieces. Elm buds, birch catkins and dandelion heads are favourite spring foods and it loves small, round and oil-rich seeds. In French gardens, lettuce seeds are favourites.

Bullfinches

Another species that tears buds is the bullfinch, which uses its short, rounded bill to tear open buds, berries, seeds and ash-keys. In late autumn and winter some bullfinches move from woodlands and thick hedgerows into farmland, orchards and gardens, but most stay in the same area all their lives. The damage that this species does to fruit buds is notorious among fruit-farmers in southern England (plums and pears are the favourites). The greatest damage appears to be in years when the crop of ash seeds is low. In England, the bullfinch is an unusual visitor to bird-tables and prefers to feed in trees rather than take seeds from the ground. On the occasions when it does feed on the ground, it seldom does so far from cover. In continental Europe, however, this species seems to feed more frequently at bird-tables and on the ground.

Canary connection

The domestic canary is descended from a species that is found in the Canary Islands, Azores and Madeira. The wild canary is a drab greenish finch related to the serin, a common European garden bird, and the bright yellow plumage of the domestic variation has been produced by careful selective breeding of the yellowest birds. The canary was introduced to mainland Europe and Britain in the sixteenth century.

Bullfinches feed on hawthorn buds.

Places to find food

A garden has plenty of places in which birds can feed naturally. In many ways it shares characteristics with woodland, in that it has different levels at which birds can find food. The trees, shrubs and flowers all provide areas to be exploited by different species.

Spotted flycatcher hovering for insects.

A treecreeper searches for tiny insects in the bark of an old apple tree, whose windfalls will provide for thrushes in winter.

A dunnock searches for insects and seeds in a flowerbed.

Swifts feeding high in the sky.

Blue tits forage for insects at
the tips of hawthorn branches.

Snails are taken from plants
by a song thrush.

A blackbird searches the lawn for worms.

Ants beneath the lawn are taken by a green woodpecker.

A hawfinch at a bird-table in Britain is an unusual sight, but they are regular visitors to bird-tables in parts of Germany and Switzerland.

Hawfinches

Another finch seen more frequently at bird-tables on the continent than in Britain, is the hawfinch. This is a large finch which is difficult to see in its woodland habit where it spends most of its time in the tree canopy. Some, however, do breed in large gardens. The hawfinch is characterised by its strikingly heavy bill and powerful muscles that are capable of cracking open olive stones with a force of over 52 kg; a remarkable achievement for a bird that weighs only 55 g. They deal with small seeds in the standard finch-like way, fitting them into the grooves in the upper mandible, but they have special adaptations to cope with the stones of olives and cherries. Early on in its life, in its first winter, a hawfinch develops two horny knobs inside each mandible in order to crack hard nuts. Until these knobs develop the hawfinch eats relatively soft food.

Greenfinches

The greenfinch is another thick-billed finch, although its bill is considerably smaller than the hawfinch's. Their large bills allow greenfinches to eat seeds of a variety of sizes – the larger ones are picked from the ground and others are taken directly from plants. Just over half of their food is found in trees. Despite being bulky birds, they can be quite agile in search of food. Their ability to perch horizontally enables them to take peanuts from hanging feeders.

Peanuts in a feeder are eaten by greenfinches.

House sparrows

The shape of a house sparrow's bill is clearly that of a seed-eater, but it eats a variety of food. In addition to seeds a house sparrow will eat other edible parts of plants – shoots, buds and berries. The house sparrow's ability to exploit human food specially provided by humans, or accidentally as rubbish, has enabled it to thrive alongside people even in the most densely populated city centres. When searching for food it words at ground-level and prefers low-growing plants. A notable exception to this feeding behaviour is when corn is ripe and sparrows perch on the ears of corn, balancing by flapping their wings, to eat it. It is possible that this habit may be responsible for recent declines in the numbers of house sparrow, which may have been affected by poisonous seed-dressings on corn.

Insect-eaters turn vegetarian

While finches are primarily seed-eaters which eat insects during the breeding season, there are several insect-eating birds which turn to a vegetarian diet in winter when insects are difficult to find.

Tits

Tits have stout bills, which are pointed for probing crevices for insects and strong enough to break through the hard outer skeletons of insects, as well as through seed-husks. In late autumn and early winter they turn to seeds, berries and nuts for the bulk of their diet. This food must fuel growth, maintain body temperature and provide the energy needed for these small birds' active lives.

Small birds such as tits lose energy faster than larger birds and as the weather becomes colder they lose heat more quickly. 'Counting the calories' for a bird's diet is a matter of keeping the intake of calories up, not down, and providing enough energy for survival. A blue tit must be busy feeding throughout the day to maintain its daily energy expenditure of about 10 calories. Since one gram of fat yields about 9 calories of energy, several grams would be needed to provide a blue tit with enough energy to survive several days without food. However, tits do not build up fat reserves, they rely on feeding daily to provide enough energy to get them through the day and the following night.

Suet wedged in the crook of a branch provides a winter meal for a nuthatch.

Tits lose weight overnight. The colder the night, the greater the weight loss because the tits use their small night-time fat reserves to compensate the heat loss. Between 5% and 10% of body weight is lost between

Winter feeding

Winter feeding may make the difference between survival and starvation. As species feed in different ways and at different heights, a variety of food should be offered at a variety of levels. A bird-table, well-stocked with seeds, fruit, bird cake, fat and kitchen scraps, hanging baskets and food scattered on the ground ensure that there is a selection for all. Remember also to provide water for drinking and bathing.

dusk and dawn. During cold weather the birds have to feed harder during the day to increase the night-time fat reserves. If food is difficult to find, the tits have serious problems and may die.

A tit's bill-shape does not enable it to crack open any but the tiniest seeds, but it can still feed on larger seeds or nuts because it has the ability to hold them steady with its feet and stab through the shells to reach the edible parts. Marsh tits, woodland birds which sometimes visit bird-tables, hold fruit in one or both feet to eat the flesh and then jab at the seed-husk with their upper mandible.

The acrobatic coal tit has a finely pointed bill with which it probes for tiny insects and spiders and, in winter, for seeds in the cones of conifers. Although coal tits will visit deciduous woodland and gardens they prefer conifer forests. To get to the seeds in cones of spruce and pine coal tits have three approaches: flying to a cone and extracting the seeds by hanging upside-down or to one side; perching above the cone and hanging down to extract the seeds from the top third of a cone; and hovering to extract seeds from fully open cones.

As insects become more difficult to find in autumn great tits increasingly depend on beech and hazel seeds. They spend much of their time feeding on beechmast on the ground until snow cover makes this impossible and they have to move to other feeding areas such as gardens. Their habit of feeding on the ground reduces competition with other tits (especially blue tits) but it can have disadvantages in periods of prolonged snow

A nuthatch carrying food.

cover. Then, tree-feeding blue tits have a better chance of survival and the food put out on bird-tables and in nut baskets becomes very important to whether individual great tits survive the winter.

Dunnocks

Another summer insect-eater which feeds on seeds during winter is the dunnock, but even in the depth of winter, insects, spiders, small snails and earthworms account for more than half its diet. It forages for seeds on the ground, very often in the cover of shrubs and hedges. It hops forward, pecking at the ground almost continuously, sometimes crouching with legs bent and body almost touching the ground as it shuffles forward. Dunnocks are sometimes known as hedge sparrows, because, superficially at least, their grey and brown plumage look rather sparrow-like – but look carefully at the bill which is much more slender than a sparrow's.

Collared doves

Another garden bird to find its food mainly on the ground is the collared dove. Its foraging behaviour emphasises its need to be on the look-out for cats and other predators. As it walks forward, it holds its head steady in a more or less constant position in relation to its surroundings, only dropping it at the last moment to pick at food. By doing this it is able to spot food and maintain all-round vision.

Nuthatches

In western Europe the nuthatch is a bird of open deciduous woodland, and it has adapted to parkland and gardens with mature trees. It is possible to see nuthatches in central Paris in Le Jardin du Luxembourg and in many gardens, where it is a popular bird-table visitor. It is another bird which transfers its attention from insects to seeds and fruit in autumn and will take a wide range of food from feeders and bird-tables.

Nuthatches are adapted to cope with food found in wood. To split a nut to reach its kernel, the nuthatch wedges it in a crevice in bark and hacks at it with its strong, pointed bill. It cannot split a hazelnut's hard shell, but can hack holes in the shell to get to the kernel. A hazelnut which has been attacked by a nuthatch can be recognised by the large, ragged hole in the shell.

The jay's bill can cope with both insects and acorns.

Great tits

If a nut has been attacked by a great tit, it has a small, neat oblong hole surrounded by tiny marks made by the bird's bill. A great tit will wedge large, hard seeds into deep crevices in the trunks of elderberries and hammer its way through the husks. Persistence is necessary for the tit intent on eating a hazelnut: it may take 10 minutes for the bird to break through the shell while holding it steady with one foot and another five minutes to eat the kernel.

Woodpeckers

To smash into well-protected food items either requires the food to be held still and attacked with the bill or for it to be smashed against a hard surface. A great spotted woodpecker uses both methods: it will hack into a tree trunk to make a crevice in which it wedges cones to hold them steady while it extracts the seeds. At regularly used feeding spots there may be a pile of discarded cones and nutshells. A hazelnut attacked by a woodpecker has a larger, more even hold than one eaten by a nuthatch. When a woodpecker smashes a pine cone to extract the seeds or a nut to extract the kernel, it will use any convenient hard surface as an anvil.

Jays

A typical woodland species which may be seen in gardens is the jay, a member of the crow family. Its comparatively long, pointed bill is heavy enough to cope both with large insects and with vegetable material. Its staple food is usually acorns. To break through the shell of the acorn, the jay holds it on a perch between both feet and bites with its bill until the shell splits. Then the bird either breaks off pieces of the kernel or stabs at it with a partly open bill to rasp off small pieces.

Storing food

When food is plentiful some birds store surplus nuts and seeds for the future. Jays begin to bury acorns when they are ripe and will recover them when food becomes scarcer later in the winter. They choose open areas, which habit is thought to have been a means by which oakwoods spread north as the glaciers from the last Ice Age retreated.

It is in harsh northern conditions that storing food is most important and among tits it seems to be less frequent in Britain than in Scandinavia. However, the garden birdwatcher can sometimes see a coal tit picking up fragments of nuts from beneath a bird feeder and flying off with them to return very quickly to collect some more. These fragments, collected without having to compete on the feeder with the larger great and blue tits, are stored either in the ground or for future use. Although storing birds recover a large proportion of the food they bury and may be able to remember the hoarding place several days later, stored items are very often used within a matter of hours.

The blackcap eats insects throughout the summer, but as autumn approaches this warbler turns to berries and soft fruits.

In autumn and winter when insects and other invertebrates become less easy to find many insect-eating birds turn to berries and fruit for food. You can add to the variety of birds in your garden by planting berry-bearing bushes and fruit trees.

Feeding on berries and fruit

Several species feed on ivy, one of the best all-year-round wildlife plants. Ivy berries are a favourite food of the wood pigeon, who uses its wings to balance as it picks the berries.

Berries and fruit form a large part of the autumn and winter diet of thrushes.
Mistle thrushes, appropriately enough, feed on the berries of mistletoe which
grows parasitically on apple trees and poplars.

The redwing is a shy winter visitor but is tempted into
gardens by ornamental berries such as pyracantha.

The fieldfare is likely to be tempted by berries
in gardens and in very hard weather will join
blackbirds, mistle thrushes, song thrushes
and starlings feeding on windfall apples.

A native of Africa and Asia, the ring-necked parakeet has become established as a breeding bird in parts of Europe, where it will visit gardens to feed on fruit.

Berries and fruit

Many insect-eating birds turn to berries and fruit for food in winter. The gardener who enjoys seeing birds as well as plants in the garden can add to the variety of birds by planting berry-bearing bushes and fruit-trees.

Elderberries, although not greatly popular with gardeners, are a favourite autumn food for many birds which eat insects throughout the summer. The spotted flycatcher adapts its insect-hunting method (*see* page 32) to feed on elderberries by hovering to pluck them from the tips of branches.

Blackcaps

The blackcap eats insects throughout the summer, but as autumn approaches, this warbler turns to a wide range of berries and soft fruits, starting with elder, among the first berries of the season, then moving on to ivy and ornamental berries such as cotoneaster.

Wood pigeons

Several species feed on ivy, one of the best all-year-round wildlife plants. Ivy berries are a favourite food of the wood pigeon. One of the larger garden birds, the cumbersome wood pigeon, uses its wings to balance as it picks berries from ivy growing up a fence.

Thrushes

Berries and fruit form a large part of the autumn and winter diet of thrushes. Mistle thrushes feed on the berries of mistletoe which grows parasitically on a number of trees, particularly apple, oak and poplar. It also takes other berries, particularly holly in Britain. Holly berries are also eaten by thrushes in May and June before they ripen. The smaller song thrush seems

Berry-bearing shrubs are excellent for attracting birds to the garden. Bright red cotoneaster berries are eaten by blackbirds and other members of the thrush family. This bird is a female.

to prefer yew of all the native British berries, but will eat many other species including haw, ivy and elder.

Pyracantha, cotoneaster and other ornamental berries are all eaten by the three common garden thrushes. In cold weather in January these bushes will also tempt the redwing, a shy winter visitor from Scandinavia, into gardens. The larger fieldfare is also likely to be tempted by berries in gardens and in very hard weather will join blackbirds, mistle thrushes, song thrushes and starlings in gardens to feed on windfall apples and pears.

Blackbirds eat the widest variety of berries and fruit: they will eat 21 different species as opposed to the song thrush's seven. Throughout autumn two-thirds of the blackbird's food is vegetable matter. Berries that ripen to a red colour are particularly attractive to blackbirds, which show a greater preference for red cherries than for white ones. They are also very fond of ripe mulberries. Birds feeding on squashy berries in autumn may test the tolerance of the most ardent bird-lover when their purplish-red droppings land on well-polished cars, stain clean washing on the line or dribble down smart white walls. Their fondness for grapes, raspberries and strawberries can cause problems for wine-growers and fruit-farmers.

Nectar

Nectar is another source of food from plants. In warmer climates it is an important source of food for hummingbirds and sunbirds. In North America hummingbirds are attracted to gardens by special feeders filled with a sugar and honey solution. Where these have been used in Europe blue tits have learned to use them with enthusiasm. Blue tits have also been seen tearing off the petals of cherry flowers and puncturing the base to reach the nectar and will eat willow catkins for the nectar. In the garden of the Seigneurie on Sark, house sparrows probe the stamens of the bottle-brush plant to reach nectar. The habit of house sparrows in stripping the petals from yellow crocuses and primulas is very puzzling. They seem to prefer plants with yellow flowers and tend to ignore the other colours. Sometimes they strip single petals from the plants and at others tear off the whole flowerhead, leaving them to lie on the ground uneaten.

A fieldfare eating rosehips. This large thrush ventures into gardens in cold weather.

Invasion by berry-eaters

The waxwing is a starling-sized bird which breeds in forests in the north of Europe and Russia and winters in southern Scandinavia and Eastern Europe with a few birds moving westwards in winter. In some winters, though, they invade western Europe in large numbers, because there is not enough food in their usual wintering-grounds. In invasion years, garden birdwatchers in western Europe are delighted to see waxwings feeding on berries in their gardens.

Insect-eaters

From the tops of trees to several centimetres below the surface of the earth there are thousands of tiny animals, which provide an important source of food for birds. At some time during the year all garden birds eat insects and other invertebrates. Even the typically thick-billed seed-eaters, such as the finches, take insects to feed their young.

Most of the invertebrates found in the garden are members of the group known as Arthropods, which contain more than 85% of the world's animal species. They are characterised by having an external skeleton of hard cuticle, known as chitin, divided into segments, some of which may have legs. The arthropods most

The surface of the ground is home to many insects and other invertebrates. All of them are potential food for birds who exploit this rich source of food, picking invertebrates from the ground, turning over leaves and probing the surface for them.

Hunting insects and other invertebrates on the ground

Song thrushes hunting invertebrates underground either run or hop in a straight line, pause to watch for movement in the grass and feed, or run on again. An earthworm is spotted as its tip protrudes above the surface.

When soil is turned over with a fork it
brings to the surface tunnelling insects,
worms, grubs and beetles, and provides a
source of food readily exploited by robins.

Blackbirds are noisy feeders; they flick
dead leaves aside with their bills to reveal
the small animals living beneath them.

likely to be encountered in the garden are millipedes, centipedes, spiders and mites, crustaceans (which include woodlice) and, of course, insects.

Other important invertebrates in gardens include earthworms and molluscs. A mollusc is characterised by its hard shell and muscular 'foot', and garden molluscs include snails and slugs (the oval shells of which are concealed beneath their slimy mantles).

Invertebrates are important sources of food for birds. Different species have adapted to use different techniques to take advantage of the great variety of invertebrate food available.

Bills and other bodily adaptations

The shape of a bird's bill gives an immediate clue to what it eats. While seed-eaters have heavy husk-crushing bills, frequent eaters of invertebrates generally have more slender and pointed bills. The shapes of these bills differ according to the prey-type each eats.

The pointed bill of the nuthatch is strong enough to hack through the shells of nuts it wedges in the crevices in tree bark and long enough to pick insects hiding in the bark. The nuthatch often descends a tree trunk head first.

Goldcrests and warblers

The tiny goldcrest feeds on minute insects and spiders which it finds high in yews and other conifers, using its fine pointed bill to pick its prey from needles, twigs and branches. Warblers, such as chiffchaffs and willow warblers, have fine bills with which they can pick insects from leaves.

Treecreepers

Some invertebrates hide in crevices in bark and must be winkled out. One of the birds best equipped to do this is the treecreeper, whose down-curved bill is finely pointed and whose long tongue is horny and tipped with bristles which help it to locate and extract insects. With its long claws and stiff tail-feathers it climbs the trunk, often in a spiral, searching for prey in the bark. When it reaches the top of the tree it flies down to the base of the next and starts to spiral again.

The finely pointed, curved bill of the treecreeper probes the crevices in tree bark in search of the small insects and spiders living there.

Nuthatches

Another trunk-feeder is the nuthatch, which picks insects and spiders from the bark with its strong, pointed bill. Over half of its food is found on the trunk, but it also searches among branches and picks food from them and from leaves that are within reach. Because, unlike the treecreeper, it can descend trees head first, it often flies from the crown of one tree to the crown of the next.

Wrens

Another prober is the wren, which has a fine, slightly curved bill. It feeds in a greater variety of places than the treecreeper, probing crevices in search of food and moving rapidly from one searching place to another. Moving along the foot of a fence it seems almost to scuttle like a small mouse.

Spiders and tiny insects which live in the corners of window frames are a source of food for blue tits, whose acrobatic abilities enable them to reach these small creatures in remote corners and cracks.

The wren often hunts for insects close to the ground, probing the bark with its fine, slightly curved bill.

Tits

The finer a bird's bill the more likely it is to feed almost exclusively on insects. However, many insect-eaters take a substantial amount of seeds and berries and even though their bills are pointed they are comparatively heavy. The bills of tits are pointed, but are stout and strong enough to cope with hard seeds in winter. The relative shortness of their bills can be a disadvantage when dealing with larger insects, but a tit will use one foot to hold a caterpillar steady while it bites off the head. When feeding young, parents will remove wings from moths and butterflies and will behead spiders.

Long-tailed tits feed mainly on small spiders and tiny insects found at the tips of leaves and on twigs, often high in trees. With their slightly curved bills, they can prise moth's eggs from clusters on branches or the underside of leaves and can also crack open seed-husks. Searching for food in precarious places at the tips of branches, Long-tailed tits need to be even more acrobatic than other tits: their stout hind toes enable them to hang from the outermost twigs and their long tails are used to help them maintain their balance.

Dunnocks

The ground-hugging dunnock picks insects and other invertebrates from the soil, but also takes seeds and berries, which accounts for its comparatively stout bill. It hops across the ground steadily, its body held horizontally and its bill pecking continually. It always moves forward and never retraces its steps.

To find insects in trees, the great spotted woodpecker will chip and strip away bark and slivers of wood as it clings to the bark with its toes, steadying its body with its stiff tail.

Blackbirds

The thrushes are generalists, particularly blackbirds, which use their longish, heavyish, fairly pointed bills to cope with earthworms, insects of various sizes, seeds, berries and windfall fruit and to forage among leaf litter.

Woodpeckers

A high proportion of a great spotted woodpecker's food is made up of insects. These may be taken from rotting wood which the woodpecker hacks away with its heavy, chisel-shaped bill, by probing the bark or by picking them from the surface of the trunk, branches or leaves. Woodpeckers' skulls are strengthened to withstand the impact of hammering into wood. Their feet have two toes pointing forwards and two pointing

backwards, which help them to cling to the surface of the bark, and stiffened tail feathers which act as props as they move up tree trunks.

Great spotted woodpeckers have tongues that extend for 40 mm, are sharply pointed to enable them to impale grubs, and also have saliva-covered bristles to which insects stick. The green woodpecker visits lawns in search of ants. It has a flat tongue which is capable of extending to more than 100 mm and which the woodpecker uses to probe ant colonies. The tongue is wider at its tip, which is flexible and capable of independent movement, has no barbs, but is covered with sticky saliva which traps ants and their grubs.

Finding insect prey

Good eyesight is needed to spot small insects at a distance and insect-eaters have comparatively large eyes and acute vision. It is difficult to make comparisons between human vision and that of those birds which have eyes on the sides of their heads. Predatory birds, such as owls and hawks, have eyes facing forward, giving them binocular vision like humans, monkeys and dogs. Most garden birds are at risk from predators and their eyes are set at the side of their heads, giving them monocular vision to the side and binocular vision in a small segment in front of them. Spotted flycatchers are sight-feeders and have large eyes, but little more than half of their prey is caught in flight. The rest is picked from the ground and from trees. Pied flycatchers, which are found in some gardens near their woodland habitat, also catch insects by sallies from a perch, but find most of their prey in trees, working methodically

Some house sparrows become adept at catching butterflies and moths. This is a magpie moth.

from the ground up the trunk. Chiffchaffs take flies by hovering and will fly from the ground in pursuit of insects. Some house sparrows have learned the hovering technique to catch damselflies in flight.

Goldcrests

Goldcrests feed on insects found on twigs in the crowns of trees but they have been seen to take advantage of insects trapped in spiders' webs by hovering and picking them from the gossamer. The spiders themselves are also prey for goldcrests which hack their eggs from branches.

Coal tits

The acrobatic coal tit will hang from a branch and closely examine leaves or pine-needles for insects. They may also move to the trunk to search for insects and spiders in the bark.

Warblers

The common whitethroat, which breeds in scrub and hedgerows, may visit gardens on the edges of villages during the breeding season or pass through on migration. It picks insects, such as small beetles and weevils from the underside of leaves.

Large well-grown gardens may even attract lesser whitethroats, which feed in taller shrubs than common whitethroats. In recent years lesser whitethroats have been breeding in large gardens in Berlin. Closely related is the inaptly named garden warbler, which is rarely seen in gardens. It is another picker of insects from leaves as are the willow warbler and the chiffchaff. All these birds are warblers and most likely to be seen in gardens if they pass through on migration, although some chiffchaffs, like blackcaps, winter in gardens, relying to a large extent on hand-outs at the bird-table.

Pied wagtails

The dashing pied wagtail is recognisable by its pied plumage and constantly moving tail. It snatches small invertebrates from the surface of a lawn while walking, and walks across water lilies to pick at aquatic insects. It darts after faster prey, taking them on the run and sometimes flying up from the ground to catch flies it disturbs from the grass. Its smart plumage and busy activity makes the pied wagtail a very attractive garden visitor.

Robins

There are several reasons for the appeal of the robin to human beings. One of them is the bird's expression with its large eyes and its sharp-eyed gaze. But however appealing these qualities may be, they are vital for the bird's survival, because its sharp eyes help it to find food. Often a robin feeds by perching a metre or so above the ground, watching for the movement of an insect or worm and flying down to take it from the ground. It then carries the food in its bill back to the safety of its perch.

The bright-eyed robin perches on a fork handle and, cocking its head, scans the surrounding ground for worms, insects and other invertebrates uncovered by a gardener's digging.

The common whitethroat is a bird of scrub, open woodland and hedgerows, visiting country gardens when they are close to its natural habitat. It feeds on insects, especially small beetles, caterpillars and weevils taken from the tips of shrub leaves.

The lesser whitethroat feeds in taller, denser shrubs and can be found in scrub and large hedges sometimes breeding in well-grown gardens and parks.

Long-tailed tits forage in small flocks of between eight and 20 birds in the tops of trees and hedgerow shrubs in autumn and winter.

The blackcap picks insects from leaves at up to a height of 20 m, sometimes hovering to pick insects from the tips of trees.

Finding insects among the leaves and branches

Insects have found ways to exploit all parts of plants from the roots to the tips of the leaves. And birds have found ways of finding these insects. Individual species of birds specialise in foraging in particular places.

When they are migrating willow warblers pass through gardens, picking small beetles, greenfly, flies and small spiders from the leaves of trees in their fine, pointed bills.

Catching flying insects

Many insects can fly, but whenever they take to the air there is danger that they will be taken by birds which have adapted to catching their prey in flight. To catch flying insects a bird needs a broad gape, which acts as a scoop, and bristly feathers around the bill, which act as a net to deflect insects into the bill. Birds specialising in feeding on airborne insects employ one of two main methods. There are swoopers, such as swallows and swifts, which catch flies at speed, and hoverers, such as spotted flycatchers, which watch for flies from a perch, fly after them, hover briefly and snap them up.

Invertebrates in the garden

Invertebrates are animals without backbones and account for 95% of all animal species. Within this group are smaller, but still broad categories: annelids include earthworms; gastropods, derived from the Greek meaning 'stomach-foot', include snails and slugs; and arthropods, whose name means 'jointed-feet', include woodlice, spiders, centipedes, millipedes and insects. All the arthropods have segmented bodies and hard body-covering. Insects have three segments: head, thorax and abdomen, and six jointed legs.

Coping with insect prey

The relatively small size of many garden birds means that some insects are too big to consume in one gulp. Tits, with their short, pointed bills, a compromise between insect- and seed-eating, cannot swallow a large caterpillar in one go, but there is so much nutritional value in it that it is worth the bird persevering to eat. Using a foot to hold the insect steady it will bite off the head with its hard jaws and reduce the larva to a manageable size. A coal tit may take up to five minutes to do this, but it may be worth the effort, which would otherwise be expended finding the equivalent amount of food. A great tit will use both feet to hold a food item down while it it bashes it with its bill.

A tiny wren at only 9.5 cm in length has to restrict itself to small food items. Any insect up to 7 mm long can be swallowed whole, but the bird has to strike anything larger against a stone to kill it and break it up. One wren was seen to break up tiny frogs before feeding them to its fledglings.

The large wings of some insects are a particular difficulty for feeding birds. A spotted flycatcher which captures a small tortoiseshell butterfly in flight will take it to a branch and remove the wings by smashing the butterfly against it. House sparrows will deal with damselflies in the same way.

The chitin of an insect's body may be so hard that it is indigestible. Birds cope with indigestible material by regurgitating it in the form of pellets. Oval pellets of the

Spotted flycatchers are expert at snatching flying insects, such as this small tortoiseshell butterfly.

Two adult and two juvenile starlings forage for insects and other small animals beneath the surface of a lawn. They walk forward, probing with closed bills which they then open to create small holes from which they pick food items.

Methods of finding prey

Birds that pick insects from the surface of leaves and branches find their prey by sight, but others use a combination of sight and hearing. Song thrushes use such a combination to detect earthworms feeding beneath the surface. Great tits will tap acorns to see if there are insect larvae in them and will leave those which are empty. They will also tear away moss and lichen to reveal prey, but most of their food is found by sight. The great spotted woodpecker apparently chooses the places on tree trunks to search for insects by tapping the trunk with its bill and listening. The insects are then found either by removing bark and uncovering them or by the bird probing with its tongue beneath the bark.

Some insects are attracted by fungi, with some species even laying their eggs in them. Birds in turn are attracted by the larvae of the insects. Both great tits and green woodpeckers will tear into fungi in search of insect larvae.

Finding insects and other invertebrates on the ground

Birds feed at various levels in the garden. Although none burrows beneath the surface in search of food, the green woodpecker inserts its bill and long, flexible tongue into ant colonies beneath lawns, and blackbirds and song thrushes snatch earthworms from just beneath the surface. One common species of earthworm feeds on the plant material which collects on the lawn and pulls it down into its burrow. It is when it is collecting the material that the earthworm is vulnerable.

The blackbird hunts by hopping or running across the lawn in a straight line, pausing for about 10 seconds with its head cocked to catch sight of the tip of the worm's body protruding through the surface or the sound of its movement. Once an earthworm has been located and eaten, the blackbird will continue to hunt in the same area because earthworms tend to be distributed in clumps. For some reason, song thrushes and female blackbirds apparently make longer runs between pauses than male blackbirds. This may be a means of avoiding competition between two similarly sized species and between the sexes of blackbirds.

Thrushes

The redwing, a winter visitor from northern Europe, feeds in loose flocks on large lawns, fields and playing fields by running or hopping in short bursts of up to five paces. It halts between each run to scan the earth, stepping forward to pick up any morsel it spots.

Another winter-visiting thrush, the fieldfare, is sometimes seen feeding in company with redwings. Its heavy bulk and stout bill enable it to turn over small clods of earth and stones in search of invertebrates as they become more active in early March.

fur and bones of small animals are produced by birds of prey, but garden songbirds also produce pellets. However, these are small, often round and almost impossible to find unless you watch the bird regurgitate the pellet. Even then these small pellets may be impossible to find. The large, hard wing-edges of great diving beetles may be found in the large, oval pellets of the grey heron. These may also contain the fur of mammals such as water voles, but they very rarely contain fishbones.

Catching insects in flight

Flying insects are a source of food for those birds capable of catching them. There are two main ways in which garden birds catch flies in flight – hovering and swooping.

The best of the hoverers is the spotted flycatcher which takes more than half of its prey in flight. In addition to small flies, butterflies and dragonflies are caught by these birds; they beat the wings off these larger insects before swallowing the head, thorax and body.

Swallows, house martins and swifts are all experts at catching flying insects, swooping on their prey and catching them in their widely gaping mouths. They have bristles on either side of their gapes to act as nests to deflect insects into their mouths. Each species tends to feed at a different level in the sky to avoid competition.

A layer of leaves on the ground provides cover for invertebrates when the weather becomes colder in autumn. Blackbirds will search among this leaf litter for food. The foraging blackbird is noisy and vigorous, flicking leaves aside with its bill or scratching them backwards with one foot to discover any animal beneath. Marsh tits will search among leaf litter for spiders, insects and seeds.

Although the snail-bashing behaviour of the song thrush is well known, this bird only seems to take snails when other food is scarce. The other four thrushes likely to be seen in gardens – blackbird, mistle thrush, redwing and fieldfare – all eat snails but none of them is quite so skilful at breaking the large shells. A song thrush will grasp the snail by the lip of its shell and hammer it hard against a stone, brick or even a pathway until the shell shatters. Once the shell has shattered, the body of the snail falls to the ground and the thrush wipes it on the ground to clean pieces of shell from its bill.

Thrushes also eat slugs, but before doing so they wipe them on grass or bare earth to remove the slime, a process which may take several minutes.

While the song thrush will search beneath vegetation for invertebrates, when feeding on the ground the larger and more wary mistle thrush avoids the shade of shrubs and sticks to the open.

Having found a snail in a flowerbed, a song thrush grips it by the lip of the shell and brings it to a paving stone. This is an anvil onto which the thrush repeatedly brings the snail downwards. As it does so it twists its head to increase the force of the impact, until the shell smashes and the body of the snail can be withdrawn.

Finding insects in trees

The trunks of trees provide plenty of places for insects and spiders to shelter. Trees whose bark has deep crevices are particularly favoured by insects and conse-quently by insect-eating birds. Native trees support the greatest number and variety of insects and the most productive is the oak. In many areas residential devel-opments, particularly those dating from before the Second World War, have been built on woodland and some garden-owners are lucky enough to have mature oaks left. In these gardens there may be both jays and nuthatches. An oak-tree trunk can support half of the species of insect recorded as being taken by the nuthatch. Its heavy, pointed bill is adapted to probing the crevices in the bark and in cold weather, when the insects and spiders are difficult to find, it will rip bark away to reach any that are hidden. The agile nuthatch can descend a tree trunk head first in a series of jerky hops. Another tree-trunk feeder, the treecreeper chooses the perpendicular or near-perpendicular trunks of trees covered with crevices in which insects can be found. It will also search on the trunks of old apple-trees and hawthorns and among the mosses and lichens on old walls. Unlike the nuthatch, it feeds almost entirely throughout the year on insects and spiders, sometimes supplementing this diet with a few pine-kernels. It always moves upwards, never heading down the trunk like a nuthatch. On the continent, the treecreeper tends to be found in conifer forests while the very similar-looking short-toed treecreeper is more likely to be seen in gardens. It tends to move more slowly, progressing in slower spirals, and is more likely to move to side branches than the treecreeper.

Tits

Although not equipped with a bill capable of breaking through thick bark, the blue tit can strip bark from the stems of hazel apparently to reveal insects and their grubs. It will also tap the stems of reeds to locate insects. Because insects are most active in summer and move higher up a tree, the birds that feed in trees tend to follow them. Therefore, they often feed higher in summer than in winter, but each species does tend to specialise at particular levels.

While the different species of tits often feed in the same area, each employs slightly different techniques and feeds in different niches, which avoids competition between them. Coal tits feed much more frequently on the ground in winter, but feed in trees to a height of 10.5 m in midsummer. More than half of their feeding in trees takes place hanging from a branch. Blue tits, which feed high in the crown of trees, spend slightly less time hanging than feeding in an upright posture, but they can change between each posture almost too quickly for the human eye. The change in posture is slower in great tits, which feed higher up in the tree than the other tits. Sometimes great tits will flutter up the outermost part of the crown picking off insects.

The marsh tit and the willow tit look very similar, but there are subtle differences in plumage and both their behaviour and voices differ noticeably. The willow tit has a pale panel on its wing, a matt black cap, a larger bib and a larger head than the marsh tit. Their names are not very accurate: the marsh tit is found in deciduous woodland and may be seen in gardens. The willow tit is less dependent on woodlands, particularly in winter, when it forages more widely than marsh tits. The willow tit is a less vigorous feeder than the marsh tit which tears at bark to reveal insects, while the willow tit feeds by sight.

Despite its name, the long-tailed tit is not a member of the tit family, but it is closely related to them and is often seen in their company in winter. Outside the breeding season long-tailed tits feed in family flocks, moving along hedgerows and through gardens very quickly, pausing only briefly to feed and keeping contact with each other through their 'tsee-tsee-tsee' calls. The tiny invertebrates on which they feed are taken mainly from the tops of shrubs and the canopy of trees. Over half of their food seems to be found on twigs, but small animals are also picked from unopened buds and the eaves of sheds and other buildings.

Catching sight of the tip of an earthworm, the blackbird strikes quickly and pulls it from the ground.

Letting others do the work

Ground-feeders are quick to exploit opportunities offered by other animals. The most obvious is the robin that perches near a digging gardener and pounces on any beetles, worms or grubs turned over with the soil. Blackbirds and song thrushes will also move in on this source of food. As moles throw up mole-hills blackbirds and robins will search for invertebrates which have been disturbed. Human footprints in the snow will uncover earth in which birds like robins can search. Outside the garden setting, several species of birds have been seen searching for food in the footsteps of wild mammals, such as badgers, wild boar and deer.

Goldcrests

Often gardens today are small and the number of mature deciduous trees in gardens is comparatively low, but conifers such as pines, yews and *Cupressus leylandii* support insects on which goldcrests feed. These tiny birds, which measure a mere 9 cm from the tip of their needle-fine bills to the tip of their short tails and weighing about 5 g, are feeders on insects and spiders picked mainly from twigs in the crown of the trees.

Redstarts

Although a bird most often seen in woodlands in Britain, in parts of continental Europe the redstart can be spotted in gardens. In the vicinity of Berlin, for example, it may be 14 times more abundant in gardens than it is in forests, and those breeding up to 2000 m in the Swiss mountains favour sites close to human habitation. It will pick insects from trunks, branches and leaves, but will also behave like a robin by flying down from a perch to pick an invertebrate from the ground and fly back to its perch to eat.

> ## Substitutes for insects
>
>
>
> In hard weather wrens, goldcrests and long-tailed tits can be attracted to the bird-table by grated cheese. Robins also take cheese. Another insect substitute is tinned cat or dog food, which the insect-eaters enjoy. But, remember, so do cats and dogs, so put it somewhere they cannot reach!

Feeding on flying insects

In summer flying insects are an important source of food for some birds, which have become effective aerial feeders. Some species feed exclusively on flying insects, for others this is one of several techniques.

There are two main ways in which garden birds forage in flight – swooping and hovering. Flying insects are usually caught in the birds' bills, but when birds of prey hunt insects they catch them in their talons and transfer them to their bills. The hobby is a small falcon, which hunts flying dragonflies and beetles, grabbing them in its talons and then transferring them to its bill.

Swoopers

Three species of exclusively aerial feeders are likely to be seen in the sky above European gardens and all use buildings for nest-sites. They swoop on their prey, taking them with their bills. All three species are superficially similar, but it is the swallow and the house martin which are closely related. The third species, the swift, does not even belong to the same Order of birds, but in an example of convergent evolution has developed similar long wings for fast flying and a wide gape with bristles on either side for swallowing insects in flight.

All three species have narrow wings which are held in a crescent and which enable them to fly very fast in pursuit of prey, but the length of tail varies. Swallows have a long tail, helping their manoeuvrability as they feed closer to the ground than the other two species. Swallows fly low over lawns to grab flies and will feed on insects hovering around the tips of branches.

The house martin forages at a higher altitude than the swallow. It approaches insects from below, catching them in an upward swoop. In summer a pair may need to catch over 1500 insects per day in order to feed their brood of four or five young.

Largest of the three is the swift, with a wing-span of up to 48 cm. It feeds in flocks on insects and airborne spiders. Over 500 species of insects have been recorded in the diet of swifts in Europe. The main groups of insects taken are aphids, flying ants, flies and beetles and the preferred size seems be 5–8 mm. Usually swifts feed in the skies close to their colonies but they will fly up to 8 km away to forage. Although they tend to feed high over built-up areas, the altitude at which they feed may be as low as 2 m or as high as 1000 m when insects are swept upwards on a thermal of warm air.

Swarming ants and beetles known as chafers attract the attention of birds which do not usually catch insects on the wing. On a warm summer day a flock of black-headed gulls may be seen spiralling upwards over towns feeding on swarming ants caught on a thermal. Joining them will be the expert aerial feeders, such as swifts, and opportunists such as starlings and jackdaws. Swarms of beetles known as chafers will attract hunting hobbies.

When flying ants swarm they provide a bonus for several species of birds which can catch them in flight. Among these are black-headed gulls, which spiral upwards in pursuit of the ants.

Hoverers

One of the best hoverers is the spotted flycatcher, which takes more than half of its prey in flight. The higher the air temperature, the more likely it is that insects will be flying and, therefore, hunted in flight by a flycatcher. When it rains, however, the insects do not fly and the birds are forced to go to the ground in search of them. Flying insects are caught by a flycatcher which darts quickly in pursuit, hovering briefly to focus on its victim before snatching it in its bill. Butterflies and dragonflies are also caught by spotted flycatchers, which beat the wings off these larger insects before swallowing the head, thorax and body. House sparrows have learned how to hover and will use this technique to capture larger insects.

Aerial feeders will take advantage of insects provided by the activities of other animals. Spotted flycatchers have been seen to take flies disturbed by a blackbird feeding on the ground and swallows feed in meadows on flies disturbed by cows. Swallows will also treat human beings in the same way as they do cattle by feeding among village cricketers whose ambling round the outfield may disturb small insects.

How birds of prey hunt

The kestrel catches prey on the ground
which it hunts by hovering, head to wind,
at about 30 m from the ground. It hangs
on rapidly moving wings, ready to detect
the slightest movement of a small rodent,
lizard, bird or large insect.

The owl most likely to be found in
a garden is a tawny owl and,
because it is nocturnal, it is much
less likely to be seen than heard.

The sparrowhawk relies on a burst of
speed and surprise to capture its prey.
The increase in people feeding garden
birds has led to some sparrowhawks
relying on feeding stations (bird-tables,
etc.) for a regular supply of food in the
form of unsuspecting sparrows, finches
and tits.

Hunters of mammals and birds

Some birds are predators on other species of birds and mammals. They have eyes capable of focusing together on their prey. To grasp fleshy, fur- or feather-covered and struggling animals they have sharp talons and to tear into the animals' flesh they have hooked bills.

Hawks and falcons, which hunt during the day, are known as raptors, from the Latin meaning to snatch. Owls, although not closely related to the raptors, share the features of their sharp talons and hooked bills, and mostly hunt at night for which they have special adaptations such as sharp binocular vision and soft plumage to muffle the sound of their flight.

Buzzards can be seen in the uplands of western Britain, or in farmland in northern Europe.

Hovering head-to-wind, a young male kestrel searches for small mammals or large insects.

Kestrels

There are two species of birds of prey likely to be seen in or from gardens during the day. The kestrel, which has adapted to urban life, catches prey on the ground which it hunts by hovering, head-to-wind, at about 30 m from the ground. As it hangs on rapidly moving wings it keeps its head absolutely motionless and its eyes focused on the ground, ready to pick up the slightest movement that might betray the presence of a small rodent, lizard, bird or large insect. Once the prey is spotted the bird drops, throwing back its wings a few metres from the ground as it brakes. The feet are thrust out to grab the prey before it escapes. Not every drop is successful and it is not unusual to see the kestrel take off again with no prey in its talons. Kestrels will also choose a prominent perch, such as a telegraph wire or a motorway gantry, from which they can scan the ground beneath for signs of movement.

Sparrowhawks

About the same size as the kestrel, the sparrowhawk has a completely different technique for taking prey. The pointed wings of the kestrel gives it sustained speed and its long tail helps it hold its position when hovering. The sparrowhawk, which has broader, rounder wings relies on a burst of speed and surprise to capture its prey. It perches in cover, swooping out to grab small birds or soars high above them stooping at a steep angle. Female sparrowhawks are larger than males, but the largest female, at 38 cm from bill-tip to tail, is a little shorter than a wood pigeon and a great deal less bulky.

Because the sparrowhawk is a predator which specialises in small birds it was seriously affected by the chemicals that dressed seed in the post-war years. These chemicals are synthetic compounds that do not break down in the environment but build up in the food web, accumulating in lethal doses among the predators at the top of the web. Since restrictions in the use of these chemicals were introduced, the sparrowhawk population has built up again. The increase in bird-feeding in the garden has attracted bird-hunting hawks into gardens to exploit the ready source of food at the bird-table. Some individuals have come to rely on feeding stations for the regular supply of food in the form of unsuspecting sparrows, finches and tits.

Buzzards

A large raptor that is common across much of northern Europe is the buzzard. It feeds mainly on small mammals. In Britain it is found in the upland areas of the west and north. Although it once appears to have been widespread across the country, its absence as a breeding bird from much of south and central England and the central lowlands of Scotland may be the result of several centuries of human persecution. However, in the West Country and mid-Wales buzzards may be seen soaring over country gardens and may even be seen perching in large trees in larger gardens. In Belgium and Holland in the winter these large birds of prey can be seen flying over towns on their journeys to the fields where they feed on rodents and birds.

Hobbies

The small, beautifully marked hobby is a falcon which breeds in Europe and migrates each autumn to Africa. It nests in trees and prefers areas where there is plenty of open space over which to hunt for insects, such as dragonflies. It will also take birds in flight and the sharp-eyed observer may spot a hobby, looking in outline rather like a large swift, hunting swallows and martins in the sky in the evening or early morning.

Owls

The owl most likely to occur in a garden is the tawny owl. But because it is nocturnal, it is much less likely to be seen than heard. It is this owl that gives the classic hooting call, and it is usually seen during daylight only

An unsuspecting vole is about to be taken by a hunting tawny owl. Hunting at night, the owl relies on its excellent hearing and eyesight to locate prey. As it nears the ground the owl brings its feet forward to snatch the vole.

Feeding in ponds

A pond is a wonderful way to attract birds to a garden. Birds will visit it to drink and to bathe and, if it has fish in it, they come to feed as well.

The kingfisher has two fishing techniques. It may perch above the water and dive (left) or hover (right) and then dive when it spots a fish.

The long legs, neck and bill of the grey heron make it an excellent fisherman. Although its long legs enable it to wade into deeper water, at most garden ponds it only has to stand on the edge, waiting for a plump goldfish to swim within striking distance. The action of taking the fish is very swift; the bird stoops very rapidly to grasp the fish in its long, pointed bill. The fish is swallowed head first to prevent its gills or fins sticking in the bird's gullet.

Other garden birds will take fish, but it is exceptional when they do. Blackbirds, which are particularly catholic in their choice of food, will take tadpoles and small fish from garden ponds. Some aquatic animals are found by the blackbird turning over stones at the water's edge.

Pellets

Some parts of a bird's diet are difficult to digest and rather than be weighed down by these slowly digested items birds will orally eject them as pellets. Pellets from birds of prey will be composed of feathers and bone. Garden birds will eject pellets of the exoskeletons of insects and very hard seeds. These are usually round, small and extremely difficult to find unless you see the bird actually producing them. Crows that have been eating corn will produce large, oblong pellets of seed-husks.

Hunters of eggs and young birds

Several species, with their own young to rear, will take the eggs and young of other species of birds. Members of the crow family are the best-known nest-robbers and they have long attracted the hatred of gamekeepers anxious to preserve their pheasant chicks. As an interest in garden birds has become more widespread, garden-bird lovers have taken an extreme dislike to crows, particularly magpies and jays.

Two black crows likely to be seen in gardens are the jackdaw (above), recognisable by its grey nape and pale eye and the larger, all-black carrion crow (below). Both eat a wide range of food, including vegetable matter, insects and carrion, and will take scraps from the bird-table.

when roosting with its body pressed tightly against a tree trunk. With its acute hearing, its huge eyes adapted to night vision and its specially soft feathers, which reduce the noise of flight, the tawny owl swoops on its prey of small rodents, frogs and insects in pitch darkness.

Smaller than the tawny owl, and more inclined to inhabit open places where there is a plentiful supply of small mammals, large insects and earthworms, the little owl may be seen in country gardens on the edges of villages. It has a particular liking for old orchards and hunts mainly at night, being particularly active from dusk until midnight, pausing for a couple of hours and resuming again until dawn. Prey is pounced on from a perch or hunted on the ground. The little owl will hop across a lawn in search of earthworms, bending forward to grasp the end of a worm and haul it from its burrow. Its tail is too short to provide much of a balance and the owl may steady itself by flapping its wings, although this does not always work and it may lose its balance and fall backwards. Sometimes the little owl will hover, but it is unable to do so with the skill of the barn owl.

A large garden with an old barn on the edge of a village may be an ideal site for the barn owl. The bulk of the barn owl's prey is mice and voles caught an hour or two before sunset and after dawn. Flying at between 0.5 and 1.5 m, rising and falling all the time the owl pauses and hovers in mid-flight searching the ground below for food. It dives forward or drops with wings raised vertically. The claws are spread as the prey is reached.

The magpie, despite taking nestlings, is not a serious pest to garden birds.

Magpies

The magpie, with its green-black plumage contrasting with patches of white and its long, unusually shaped tail, is a beautiful bird, and, if it were not for its habit of taking the eggs and young of songbirds, it would be welcomed in most gardens. In reality only a small proportion of a magpie's diet consists of the eggs and young of songbirds, if for no other reason than the fact that these are a seasonal food. Adult magpies feed mainly on grain and fruit in the winter and on ground-living invertebrates in summer. Young magpies in the nest are fed on invertebrates, such as beetles and caterpillars, and rarely more than 1% of their total intake is made up from the eggs or nestlings of songbirds. Even though some magpies in suburban gardens may seem to take a high number of songbirds, their effect on the populations of other birds is almost certainly not serious. If it were, the increase in the magpie population would have been matched by a decrease in songbird populations and this has not happened. Its size and striking patterned plumage makes the magpie noticeable and the most obvious predator in the garden, which means that the failure of any nest will be blamed on it.

Magpies learn very quickly and have a curiosity which leads them to find new sources of food. They may be attracted to investigate nests if they see someone peering into a bush at a nest. Some magpies have learned that papier-mâché cartoons left on doorsteps by the milkman mean hens' eggs and have raided these despite being unable to see what the cartoons contained. This happened so often in one town in Yorkshire that customers left out plastic bowls which the milkman put over the egg-boxes, but sometimes even these were dislodged by the magpies.

Great spotted woodpeckers

Some bird nests are beyond the reach of magpies or jays. However, hole-nesting birds, such as tits and nuthatches, are at risk from the great spotted woodpecker. This striking and usually welcomed visitor to the garden will hack at the small opening of a nestbox to enlarge it enough to poke its head in and remove the helpless young.

Predators and prey

Natural predators rarely have a damaging effect on the populations of their prey, because the predator has a vested interest in the success of its prey species. If it causes the prey to become extinct it will lose a source of food. Where the population of a prey species has been reduced to very low numbers by other causes, a predator could be responsible for the coup de grâce and predators may have effects on local populations of their prey. Nevertheless it is usually the number of prey which affects the number of predators. If there is a shortage of prey the numbers of young predators reared is smaller and many individuals may die from starvation.

Fish-eaters

A pond is a wonderful way of attracting birds to a garden. Birds visit it to drink and to bathe. And they may also come to feed at it as well. Several species of garden birds are opportunist enough to take aquatic insects, worms, small fish and tadpoles from garden ponds. Blackbirds will wade among the shallows at the edge of a pond in search of flatworms and water snails and will take any small frogs, tadpoles and newts that come within reach. Even the tiny wren will take small minnows and goldfish.

There are two striking-looking birds which may be welcomed in some gardens, but will certainly not be welcomed in others. The reason is that each is a specialist in catching fish and may visit garden ponds to take goldfish. The grey heron is striking for its size, standing a metre high, and the kingfisher, although much smaller (scarcely bigger than a house sparrow), is striking for its colours. Both have similar dagger-shaped bills to grasp and hold slippery fish.

Grey herons

The long legs, neck and bill of the grey heron make it an excellent fisherman. Although its long legs enable it to wade into deeper water, at most garden ponds it only has to stand on the edge, absolutely motionless, waiting for a plump goldfish to swim within striking distance. The action of taking fish is lightning-swift, the bird stooping very rapidly to grasp a fish in its long, pointed bill. It swallows the fish head first, because it

goes down better that way: a fish swallowed tail first might get stuck by the fins or gills in the bird's throat. The smaller the fish the faster it is swallowed. Once the heron has swallowed the fish it steps to the edge of the pond and dips its bill in the water, presumably to wash off any slime that might have come from its prey.

Kingfishers

The bill of a kingfisher is similar in shape to a heron's but is much smaller. The kingfisher has two fishing techniques – perch-and-dive and hover-and-dive. In the first, it perches on a branch with its bill pointing downwards and its eyes looking along the bill at the water for the movement of the fish. When a fish is sighted the bird dives at a sharp angle and grabs the fish in its bill. When hunting from a hovering position the kingfisher keeps its head still and looks along its bill, dropping when a fish is seen. To be successful the kingfisher has to allow for the distortion caused by the water. The bird flies to a perch and rearranges the fish in its bill so that it can be swallowed head first.

Brightly coloured goldfish in a garden pond are easy prey for such expert fishermen as herons and kingfishers and they will return to the source of supply until it runs out. This is a very good example of predators having a marked effect on their prey in a limited area. Since both species tend to visit gardens in the early hours they are often not seen and the only evidence of

Providing water for birds like this great tit to drink all through the year is one way in which gardeners can help birds.

To drink, a swallow skims low over the surface of a pond to scoop water into its bill.

their presence is a dwindling fish population. Both birds are protected by law and therefore the only action the pond-owner can take is to prevent the birds from catching the fish. Plenty of places where the fish can hide will help. Herons will be deterred by bamboo canes set at one-metre intervals around the perimeter of the pond with a string between each at about a metre's height. Don't make the string taut, because it might be a very convenient perch for a kingfisher.

To make the pond completely bird-proof you need to cover it with wire mesh, but as well as deterring unwelcome fishing species it will also prevent other birds from drinking and bathing. Try to leave a shallow patch uncovered for them, because there are interesting aspects of bird behaviour which you should have plenty of opportunity to observe if you have a garden pond.

Stealing food

Some birds learn that food is often more easily obtained by letting someone else find it and then robbing them. Garden birds may rob from members of the same species when they are feeding in flocks and they can be unscrupulous in pirating food from members of other species.

When members of the thrush family feed together the blackbird may steal worms from the song thrush and the redwing. Blackbirds may also steal snails from song thrushes, but they wait until the thrushes have smashed the shells.

Aggression when feeding is not always a matter of piracy. It may be aimed at removing competition. The mistle thrush and fieldfare, are the most aggressive towards other thrushes. A fieldfare will take up a feeding territory in a garden and drive away any blackbirds that might compete in the depth of winter for any berries on bushes, old apples and pears or the few invertebrates available in winter. Similarly, blackbirds dominate other blackbirds, redwings and song thrushes. Redwings seem to drive off only song thrushes, which seem to be dominated by all the other species.

Drinking

Animals need to drink to replace the moisture which is lost from their bodies. In the case of birds this loss occurs through evaporation from their skin and lungs. They neither sweat nor produce liquid urine. They only need to drink when their food does not contain sufficient liquid to replace the moisture lost from their bodies.

Most garden birds drink by sipping water in their bills and then raising their heads to swallow the liquid. Doves, represented in the garden by the feral pigeon, collared dove and wood pigeon, dip their bills into the water, suck it into the crop and when the crop is full raise their heads to swallow the water.

Swallows and house martins use their flying skills to drink by swooping low over the water's surface and scooping the water with their lower mandible.

Bird-table behaviour

The great tit dominates the other tits
and will drive coal tits from a nut feeder.

Boisterous behaviour by starlings helps them to dominate the bird-table hierarchy. When a flock of starlings descend they leave little chance and little room for other birds to feed.

Male house sparrows are aggressive towards other bird-table users such as this greenfinch.

Birds' defence against predators

Surprise is vital to most hunting predators and one of the defensive techniques employed by the birds that are prey is to draw the attention of other birds to the presence of the predator. A flying sparrowhawk will be attacked by starlings, which fly and swirl around it, apparently trying to confuse it. The tightness of starling flocks may also have a value on the principle of safety in numbers: the greater the number of birds, the less chance each individual has of being the one that is caught.

Mobbing

A predator which is perched or on the ground may be mobbed by songbirds. Owls are particularly susceptible to attack by small birds if they are discovered during the day. The birds make a considerable noise and the mob may consist of several species. Because mobbing often seems to take place during the period when young are leaving the nest, it has been suggested that the adults attack a predator in order to imprint its shape on the minds of the young. But if this is the case, what do the birds gain by being so noisy?

In the case of nocturnal owls being mobbed in the daytime, it does seem that the small birds have the

The neighbour's cat stalks a male pied wagtail. Cats are by far the most serious predator on garden birds. If reasonable cat owners keep their pets indoors for a couple of hours in the early morning and before dusk, then garden birds have some chance to feed unmolested. Wire fences and thick thorn or holly hedges are deterrents. If cats come through a hole in the hedge, block it with brambles.

predator at a disadvantage. Mobbing may occur because of a need for 'the worm to turn' occasionally or because the small birds find themselves confused between their desire to flee and their need to attack.

As well as birds of prey, predatory mammals and snakes are mobbed. A tabby cat sitting on a branch up against the tree trunk giving a rather owl-like impression will attract the attentions of small birds, and a hunting cat on the ground may also be mobbed. It may be that the mobbing makes so much noise that it attracts other predators larger than one being mobbed which will chase the latter away. Certainly in the case of a cat in the garden, the cries of small birds will draw the attention of human beings, whose reaction may be to deter the cat.

Mobbing can, however, be a high-risk strategy. By drawing attention to themselves the birds can be at risk from other predators. When breeding, if songbirds

Imitation as defence

Small birds may make themselves out to be something other than what they are in order to deter predators. When its nest is threatened, the female great tit makes a sharp hissing noise like a snake or a weasel. The effect is to surprise the predator and may even frighten it away. Whether this hissing is in imitation of a snake or of a threatening weasel is a matter of debate. Certainly in Britain, where snakes are not common, weasels are a greater threat to great tits, but the Aesculapian snake in central France and the ladder snake in Spain and Portugal are expert tree-climbers and add nestlings to their main diet of small mammals.

fly from cover to attack a jay, they draw attention to themselves. Rather than flight, the response of the jay may be to search the cover until it finds the nest.

Stoats exploit this mobbing tendency and songbirds' natural curiosity by performing acrobatic 'dances' to attract the birds' attention, pouncing when one of them approaches too closely.

Near the vicinity of their nests, songbirds become very aggressive in defence of their eggs and young. The normally shy mistle thrush will fearlessly attack cats and even humans in defence of its young and will even take on marauding crows. In Central Europe, fieldfares have been to seen to dive-bomb a perched predator, splattering it with faeces.

A mistle thrush threatens a predator by calling and fluffing its feathers to make itself look larger. This normally shy bird can be very bold in defence of its young.

Sitting tight

Aggression, as demonstrated in mobbing and attacking predators, is not the only strategy for dealing with predators; sitting tight can also be effective. Sometimes this is accompanied by an alarm-call, which could risk attracting the predator's attention, but the call of several species is ventriloquial, lessening the risk of discovery. The bird giving the ventriloquial alarm-note is likely to sit tight, while other members of the flock or, better still, other species, take evasive action and draw the hawk's attention away from the caller. The thin 'tsee' alarm call is shared by several species including blackbirds, great tits, blue tits and chaffinches.

The alarm-calls of blackbirds differentiate between the sources of danger. Adults warn their young of the presence of foxes, cats and other predators on the ground with a single-syllable call, variously rendered as 'pook', 'kop' or 'djuck', which is repeated until the threat has moved away. If the predator is a bird of prey the call is the 'tsee' described earlier and similar to that of other songbirds.

Tits also have a repertoire of alarm-calls. These calls are an important part of the language of birds and different calls may convey different information. For example, the reaction of nestlings to certain types of call will be to keep quiet so that the nest's existence is not given away to approaching predators. Six types of churring call have been identified in great tits and each is associated with different situations, but which may change from type to type as the situation changes.

Do not disturb

If you are being scolded by a bird, making a repetitive alarm-call, it thinks you are a predator and it may have young in the vicinity. Move off as quickly as possible. If you accidentally disturb birds in the nest and they 'explode' out of it, collect up the young birds and put them back in the nest, covering it with your hand, until they calm down. Then leave the nest area as quickly as possible.

Distraction displays

Another protective technique is the distraction display in which the parent attempts to draw the predator away from the nest. This is a device usually associated with ground-nesting waders, but some garden birds will also employ it from time to time. Single blackbirds have been seen to flop down in front of cats or people and flutter just above the ground as if they were injured. Song thrushes will hold their wings half-open and stagger along the ground as if hurt. The predator may be distracted by the prospect of feeding on a full-grown adult, whose injury will make it easier to catch.

A bird may regard a human being taking an interest in its nest as a potential predator and this may provoke an anti-predator response, particularly if the young are handled and give a distress call. Despite its small size, the blue tit will dive close to a person inspecting a nest box and make a buzzing call. The objective may be to distract the predator by presenting an apparently easy target. Blue tits will also feign injury and flutter among the branches to draw the predator away.

Protective colouring

The pattern of its plumage often helps a garden bird to protect itself against predators. The best-known type of protective patterning is cryptic colouring which enables the bird to merge with its background. Another pattern of protection comes from the combination of a bird's overall colouring, so that the bird's outline is obscured. Each of these depends on the bird remaining still until danger has passed.

Much of the dunnock's life is spent on the ground in search of food. There it is vulnerable both to ground predators, such as cats and weasels, and to birds of prey. Its protection is its dusky grey plumage, making it difficult to pick out as it skulks in the shadows of bushes and other garden plants. When danger threatens the bird freezes and merges with its shadowy background.

The contrast between the pale underparts and the dark back of the treecreeper disrupts its outline when viewed in profile as it climbs up the trunk of a tree in search of insects and spiders. However, when the bird is aware of danger it flattens itself against the tree trunk and relies for protection on the camouflage of its dark-streaked, brown back merging with the tree bark.

Tadpoles are food for many other animals and to prevent a decline in the frog population at least two offspring of every pairing must survive to reach maturity. To achieve this a female may spawn thousands of eggs.

When a bird is incubating eggs or brooding young in an open cup-nest it is vulnerable and needs to be well camouflaged. The bird settles itself as far down in the nest as it can so that only its head, back and tail are visible. In the majority of garden species, females do all or most of the incubation and because of this are often better camouflaged. For instance, the male chaffinch is brightly marked compared to his mate, whose plumage is similarly patterned but in a combination of olive-browns and greens rather than the brighter red, russet and blue-grey of the male. Although the male helps to feed the young, it is the female alone that incubates the eggs, her olive-green back and brown head merging with the mosses in the nest.

When the young chaffinches fledge they too have camouflaged plumage similar to their mother's. When they first leave the nest these cryptically coloured young seek the refuge of dense cover, remaining motionless and silent except when the parents arrive with food and the young must call to draw their parents' attention to them.

Even among the more brightly coloured species the young are more cryptically plumaged than their parents. Young green woodpeckers lack their parents' red heads, and have speckled, duller green plumage than that of the adults. Speckling on the back and wings seems to help to camouflage birds on the ground and is found among recently fledged thrushes, robins and spotted flycatchers.

Protecting themselves against birds

Any animal that is the prey of another needs to ensure that it can outbreed its predators. If it did not manage this, all members of the species would quickly be eaten and the species would rapidly be extinguished. The animals at the top of the food chain tend to rear fewer

It is difficult to pick out the dusky grey plumage
of the dunnock as it skulks in the shadows cast
by bushes and other garden plants.

When a great spotted woodpecker arrives in the garden, its black-and-white plumage and red markings make it look very obvious, but this colouring makes the bird difficult to see among the bare branches of a tree against a pale sky.

Another disruptively coloured bird is the magpie, which stands out brightly against the green of a lawn, but with its black-and-white plumage and long tail the magpie can easily be missed when it is perched high up in bare branches.

Protective colouring

The pattern of its plumage often helps a garden bird to protect itself against predators.

In a pair of chaffinches it is the female (right) that incubates the eggs, and she, therefore, needs to be more cryptically coloured than her mate. When she broods the young, she appears to merge with her nest in the shadowy crook of a branch.

Disruptive colouring

While some garden birds such as the dunnock rely on cryptic colouring, others combine this with disruptive colouring which disguises the bird's outline. The treecreeper, whose back is delicately mottled to camouflage it against a tree trunk, has a breast and underparts of the palest grey. When it is seen in profile, the shape is disrupted so that at first glance it may not be recognisable as a bird and may even look like a piece of torn bark. This may give the treecreeper precious moments in which to escape a predator.

The caterpillar of the mottled umber moth is patterned and shaped like a twig. When danger threatens, it freezes.

young than those farther down the chain. Generally speaking the most preyed-on animals produce very large numbers of young. A pair of golden eagles, which are long-lived, will rear one young eaglet in year, while a frog may lay as many as 4000 eggs in her spawn.

In addition to breeding prolifically, prey animals have developed other defence mechanisms, some of which are similar to those adopted by birds and others very different. Many reptiles, amphibians and invertebrates on which birds might feed in gardens are well camouflaged. A common lizard on a rockery might pass unnoticed as it basks in the sun and common frogs are found in a range of shades of brown and green. Most gardeners know it is easy to overlook a frog in a

The peppered moth gains protection from being patterned like pale lichen.

Its buff-coloured head and wing-tips give the buff-tip moth the appearance of a birch twig.

flower bed until it moves. For as long as it stays still its camouflage is sufficient to protect it and when it springs to life the predator is surprised and the resulting momentary pause may allow enough time for the frog to escape to cover.

Caterpillar camouflage

The caterpillars of moths and butterflies are often very well camouflaged as they munch their way to maturity. In their larval stage insects are devoted to eating. Their bodies are soft, the hardest part being the jaws, which are efficient devices for reducing their food to manageable chunks.

The geometer moths have larvae that take the concept of camouflage to the extreme, not just merging with the background but looking like part of it. The typical geometer moth caterpillar has legs at the front of its body, directly behind the head and double claspers at the tail. To move, it bends its body and inches along a twig. Its colouring matches the plant on which it feeds and when it detaches its front end from the branch its body looks like another twig. At rest the caterpillar again looks like a twig, even to the extent in some species of having bud-like nodules on its body.

Insects are particularly vulnerable to birds and have developed various defences to ensure the survival of some individuals. The peppered moth is a geometer, the twig-imitating caterpillars of which feed on a variety of trees and shrubs in gardens and woodland. The moth itself takes its name from its colour and pattern – a white insect speckled with dark marks – and when the moth is at rest on a patch of lichen on a tree it becomes almost invisible. It also exists in a melanic, almost black form, which appears to have become more common in the last century in industrial areas where industrial pollution killed the lichens, and the smoke blackened buildings and trees. The camouflaged melanic form survived the attentions of birds better in these areas than the peppered form and is now more common.

The shape, colour and pattern of the buff-tip moth make it resemble a small, broken birch twig. Several species mimic dead leaves and are camouflaged to merge with the trunks and branches of the trees on which they are found. The privet hawkmoth has an abdomen attractively striped in black and pink, but this is rarely seen by people, because when this moth is resting its forewings, shaded from dark to pale brown, are drawn over its body and it lies well hidden against the bark of the privet, lilac or ash on which it lays its eggs. The caterpillars of the privet hawkmoth are bright green, matching privet leaves, with their outlines broken by a series of diagonal brown and white stripes.

Colours that warn

Animals that sting, are poisonous or just horrid-tasting are avoided as food by many birds. From the prey's point of view it is important that the predator is warned that its prey is potentially unpleasant, if not lethal. Therefore, some species have adapted colours that are a recognisable warning to predators. These are bright and obvious, usually yellow and black in stripes, but warning colours may also be red and black and come in spots.

Wasps are obvious examples of stinging insects with warning stripes. While some birds ignore them, others, such as the spotted flycatcher, have learned to remove the stings either by rubbing the wasp's abdomen against a branch so that the sting is detached or by bashing the body against the branch for up to 15 seconds.

The bright yellow- and black-striped caterpillars of the cinnabar moth take in toxins from the ragwort on which they feed and are therefore left alone by birds.

While the knowledge that yellow- and black-striped insects are potentially dangerous may be learned, it

Birds respond to the black-and-yellow warning colours of this harmless hoverfly.

The wasp beetle displays warning colours even though it is harmless to birds.

would appear to be innate in some species at least, for example, blue tits reared in captivity refuse to eat any insects displaying warning colours and great tits refuse beetles with warning coloration and are very quick to learn that moths with warning colouration are unpalatable. It has been suggested, however, that the bird may be able to differentiate between the palatable and unpalatable by smell alone.

Some harmless insects have adopted warning colours. This is known as batesian mimicry and is most obviously found in various species of hoverflies. These are the two-winged flies that hover around plants in gardens and look remarkably like wasps or bees. Unfortunately they are often swatted by human beings fearful that they are wasps. Some species of hoverfly are in reality very helpful to the garden as they consume large numbers of aphids.

Camouflage and warning

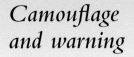

The great crested newt has a black back and when viewed from above is well camouflaged against damp earth. However, if it is viewed from below, either in the water or if it is turned over accidentally, it displays an orange-yellow belly spotted with black. This is a warning that its skin contains a toxin, which, if not lethal, will leave predators with a particularly unpleasant sensation.

As a grass snake approaches it, a common toad puffs itself up to an unswallowable size.

Surprise techniques

Some insects combine camouflage with a technique known as flash-colouring. The forewings of the red underwing moth are mottled grey, providing excellent camouflage when the moth is at rest, but if the insect is disturbed it opens its wings and flashes its bright red underwings. The pursuing bird is surprised and may pause very briefly before following the fleeing scarlet wings. However, when the moth comes to rest the red disappears and the bird may be confused enough to lose interest.

Several butterflies and moths have 'eye' patterns on one or both sets of their wings. In the case of butterflies, which rest with wings held upright, the sudden opening of their wings to display a pair of 'eyes' may surprise a predator long enough for the butterfly to make its escape. The eyes may have another function; that of distracting the bird from the body of the insect to its wings. A butterfly can survive with a small piece taken out of its wing, where it would not survive if the bird had chomped its body. It is not uncommon to see

Inflation for survival

A common toad, when confronted by a predator, will inflate its body by as much as 50% and stand on tiptoe to make itself look larger and more frightening. The toad's skin secretes a poison which can have unpleasant, and even lethal effects on other animals, but some magpies and carrion crows have learned to disembowel toads and leave the rest of the body uneaten.

peacock butterflies late in the season with triangular tears in the wing where a bird has been misled.

Animals that are eaten by birds use several forms of defence – flight, threat, cryptic colouring, warning colouring, mimickry of another animal, flash colouring and hiding. They will also avoid the attentions of birds by being active at night when few birds are.

Breeding

Courtship, nesting and incubation

Animals are driven by a desire to pass their genes on to future generations. The business of breeding leads birds to complex behaviour to ensure the survival of an individual's genes. A female can be certain that her eggs will contain her own genes, but for each male there is a risk that his mate's eggs might be fertilised by another male. He must, therefore, follow strategies that deter other males and keep his mate safe from the attentions of passing opportunists. These strategies are not always successful and some eggs of garden birds seem to be fertilised by intruding males. Once the eggs have been laid, the parents have the task of ensuring that enough of their young survive to carry their genes forward to future generations.

Few of the young are likely to survive long enough to be able to breed, because for the population of a species to remain stable there only needs to be the same number of breeding birds each year. Breeding numbers are limited by the available nesting territories and the numbers of birds that survive from one season to the next.

The time to breed

Because the human life cycle is long, with European couples generally having two or three offspring and a life expectancy of over 70 years, it is quite difficult to come to terms with the shortness of the life cycles of most small songbirds. In an oak woodland where there is plenty of food a pair of great tits may rear two clutches of a dozen eggs in a summer and they may be dead by the next.

The best time to have young in the nest is when food is most plentiful or most easily obtainable. Most birds time their breeding season so this happens. Chaffinches, which feed their young on small insects, time their breeding so they have young in the nest when caterpillars are abundant. This gives them a relatively short breeding season and in southern England this generally

occurs over six weeks in April and May. Goldfinches, which feed their young mainly on seeds, have a longer breeding season, but tend to breed slightly later than other finches so that they reach a peak in June and July.

There are also variations in the timing of breeding of the specialists in aerial feeding. Swallows, which feed on small flying insects, breed slightly earlier than house martins, which take the larger insects that emerge later. Last to breed are swifts, which feed on high-flying insects that are abundant in mid-summer. Swifts do not arrive in northern Europe until the latter part of May and lay their eggs so that hatching coincides with the insects' abundance in June.

There is a practical consideration to the timing of breeding of birds of prey. Kestrels, which are hunters of small rodents, breed in April, so that when the young hatch the vegetation is still short enough to make hunting relatively easy. Sparrowhawks are hunters of birds and breed a few weeks later so that their young hatch as the bulk of young songbirds fledge.

Since there may be weeks or even months of breeding activity before the young hatch, the breeding pair would seem to have some predictive ability. This is

In winter the male chaffinch (below) is relatively drab, but its plumage has become brighter by spring because wear on the tips of the feathers reveals a more intense colour and the bill colour changes from pale to dark. Similarly, this male bullfinch (above) has a brighter plumage in spring.

based on increasing day length and is modified by weather conditions and lack of food. There are also physiological changes in birds. Outside the breeding season their sex organs are small, but as days lengthen in the first part of the year they begin to grow rapidly. When they are fully mature they may have grown a thousand times. This is the point at which copulation and egg-laying take place. However, if weather conditions are bad, breeding may be delayed.

The songbirds in gardens tend to look brighter in spring. The house sparrow develops a black bib and the starling's plumage acquires a sheen. This results from wear on the fine, soft feather tips. As they wear, they reveal the brighter colours. Other birds acquire breeding plumage by a partial moult, for example, the black-headed gull's chocolate brown face and head feathers grow in spring.

Swifts nest in colonies in towns and villages and perform aerial social displays in which several fly at roof-top height screaming around the nest area.

Territory

To rear a family a pair of songbirds must have a sufficient supply of food within easy reach of the nest. They therefore establish a territory in which they can nest and which will provide enough food to sustain the young until they can fly and range farther afield in search of food. Maintaining a territory, which is defended against trespassers, is a way of reducing competition between members of the same species.

Although territories are most frequently associated with the breeding season, birds may hold areas in which they feed and from which they drive others. A fieldfare may in very hard weather lay claim to a single berry-laden cotoneaster and drive away other fieldfares

and other thrushes. Robins hold larger winter territories from which they will drive all other robins. By sticking to an area that it knows well the individual is more likely to survive, because it knows the places where there may be danger, such as cats, and places of safety in which to hide if danger threatens.

It is at the beginning of the breeding season that many species become highly territorial and defend areas in which they eat, sleep and breed. The territory needs to be large enough to provide food to sustain both members of the pair throughout egg-laying, incubation and then to the period during which the young, unable to fly, are confined to the nest.

Within a species the size of territories may vary with the availability of food. If food is plentiful the territory does not need to be as large as one where food is more scarce. This means that birds of the same species occupying different habitats may have territories of different sizes. Thus a great tit's territory in a garden with mature oak trees and plenty of caterpillars on which to feed the young, will be smaller than one in a garden where the main food has to be greenflies. To obtain the same nutritional value from greenflies as from caterpillars the tits must collect many more individuals.

Birds like the house martin and swallow, which may travel many thousands of miles in a year to their African wintering grounds and back, also have to find food within easy flying distance of their nests when there are eggs to incubate and young to rear. However, because they specialise in eating flying insects, which are not confined to one small area, they do not need to maintain feeding territories. Indeed, in the case of house martins, which feed on swarming insects there are advantages in finding food in flocks. However, there is still the need to defend nests and mates from the attentions of other birds of the same species. House martins, which usually breed in small colonies and may nest within metres of each other, maintain territories of about 10 cm from the nest-hole. Only the tiny area in the vicinity of the nest is defended and, as this contains no food resources, the purpose of the territory is to drive away rivals for the territory-holder's mate.

Suitable nest-sites are an important factor in a bird's choice of territory. Sufficient food to sustain the family until the young have fledged is not enough if there are no suitable nest-sites and the garden owner who wishes to encourage birds to nest must make sure that there are suitable places for them to nest.

It is easy to think that the birds that nest in a particular garden regard that garden as their territory, but to birds fences and walls provide possible nest-sites, places from which to sing, feeding opportunities and perches rather than boundaries. The birds' territories will not, therefore, be confined to a single garden and their boundaries will probably not coincide with walls or fences, but will tend to be limited by the extent to which the bird's song can be heard from regularly used song perches, and by the points where the territory-holder drives off intruders. The actual boundaries with the next territory may therefore be rather fluid.

The mistle thrush chooses a high perch from which to deliver its fluting song. It chooses an exposed perch and will often sing when it is raining.

Advertising territory with song

Garden birds usually announce their possession of a territory with song, which may be as elaborate as the blackbird's or as rudimentary as the house sparrow's. However, the magpie does not sing at all. Instead it declares its possession of a territory by sitting on prominent perches, while the sparrowhawk does it by flying above its territory.

The mechanism that songbirds have for producing vocal noises is different from that used by other animals including human beings, but, like the human voice, bird sounds are created by air flowing from the lungs being vibrated through a system of membranes. The larynx, which contains a mammal's vocal chords, is not present in birds instead they have an organ known as the syrinx. The complex arrangement of muscles, and variations in the force with which the air is expelled, result in the variety of pitch, loudness and notes to be heard in bird song.

Song enables males to proclaim their ownership of a territory and may also attract females. Birds recognise other individuals by their songs. Males holding adjoining territories recognise the songs of each other and, if a territory changes ownership the neighbours will react differently to the newcomer, by moving towards the newcomer to emphasise their own possession of territory. Similarly, they will take steps to defend their territories if a neighbour begins to use new song posts.

When faced with an intruder to his territory the male great tit puffs up his breast and sways his head to show his white cheeks. Two birds may perform this display for 10 minutes.

During the breeding season the male will patrol his territory, moving from one perch to another to deliver his song. Songbirds tend to have repertoires of songs; blackbirds may have up to 100 song types. By varying the repertoire a singing bird may be giving the impression that there is more than one singing male present, thus deterring any potential rivals, which might be persuaded that the area is too crowded to be worth trying to set up a territory.

One of the songbird virtuosi in the garden is the wren. This tiny bird has a full-throated song that sounds as though it might come from a much larger bird. This song is the fastest of any bird, too fast for the human ear to pick out the individual notes. Only when the song is recorded and played at a quarter of its normal speed do the notes become clear to the human ear.

Birds learn their songs from hearing other birds of the same species singing. The development of song in chaffinches has been studied in detail and experiments have shown that when they began to sing, birds raised as nestlings in a soundproof aviary produced songs that were different from the normal comples song of adult chaffinches. In the wild, young males after fledging sing a muted rambling subsong and do not sing again until the following spring when they sing a more complex version of the subsong. As the young male takes up a territory his song becomes similar to the songs of neighbouring males.

The idea of male birds serenading their mates has a long history in songs and verse, but just how great a role bird song plays in sexual attraction is not clear. The shyness of females makes the study of their response difficult. However, it does seem that among sedge warblers those males with the most complex songs attract mates before their rivals, although there may also be other factors influencing this.

Communicating using other sounds

Not all birds rely on their voices to communicate. Perhaps the best known of mechanical bird sounds is the great spotted woodpecker drumming its bill against a tree trunk or post. Both sexes create these sounds. They may be used to advertise territory, to attract a mate or as an aid to pair-bonding. Drumming is mostly heard during the first half of the year. Its rapidity and length may vary between individuals and they do seem to be able to recognise the drumming of their mates and of their neighbours. The frequency of the drumming appears to increase as the breeding season progresses, reaching a peak before egg-laying, when there may be 10 drumming series within a minute.

The stiff pinions of a woodpecker's wings make a faint whirring sound in flight. This appears to intensify when there are disputes over nest-sites and one bird chases another away. The wood pigeon also uses its wings to produce a sound when it performs a display-flight. Early in the season, when birds are disputing territories, the pigeon will give its cooing song, take off, rise to between 20 and 30 m, clap its wings at least once and glide down with tail outspread to a perch where it sings again. There is debate whether the loud clap is created by the wings touching at the end of the upstroke or whether it is a whip-like crack caused by the downward stroke.

Advertising territory using displays

While song is a long-range means of communicating to other birds its possession of a territory, at close quarters this message is reinforced by visual displays aimed at any intruding bird of the same species. Territories are usually defended against intruders of the same species, but sometimes, other species may be attacked where they have very similar feeding or nesting requirements.

Displays, which may sometimes be accompanied by calls, are a series of postures and body movements. This

Not all bird sounds are created vocally. The great spotted woodpecker drums its bill against a tree trunk to advertise its territory.

The dawn chorus

During the 20 minutes or so before the sun rises there is the dawn chorus, in which each species starts to sing with great intensity in a seemingly fixed order. First to sing is the nightingale, which in England is only likely to be heard in southern country gardens bordering suitable scrub or coppiced woodland. Next to sing is the skylark, a bird that may be heard in the sky above gardens bordering open fields. Then come the robin, song thrush and blackbird, followed by the willow warbler and blackcap. One theory put forward for the existence of the dawn chorus is that in the pre-dawn silence each bird sings to re-assert its territorial proprietorship and if a territory-owner does not sing the other birds assume it means that he has died in the night and that there is a vacancy. This is an opportunity for any males of that species not holding a territory to move in.

body-language may be very complex and is often deliberately conspicuous and exaggerated so that the meaning is quite clear.

When faced with an intruder the territory-holder begins an aggressive display. The male great tit performs a display in which his head is held upright and his breast expanded. The head sways from side to side to expose first one white cheek and then the other. One of the most aggressive garden birds is the robin, the displays of which are aimed at making it look bigger and at concentrating attention on its red breast.

These displays can change from aggressive postures to real aggression and sometimes the birds may come to outright blows. Both robins and dunnocks have been seen fighting to the death, but this is a rare occurrence. More often one or other of the posturing birds backs down either by responding with a submissive posture or by displacement activity.

The robin sings to proclaim his territory to other males, at the same time as enticing a female to join him.

Courtship displays

A courtship-feeding greenfinch stands upright and pushes seeds in to the female's open bill as she crouches with wings fluttering making faint begging calls.

Both sexes of goldfinches crouch on a perch and pivot from side to side on their legs, lowering their wings to show more of the yellow wing-bars and puffing their cheeks to expand the bright red cheeks.

The submissive postures minimise the size of the bird and often involve crouching and turning the bill away from the aggressor.

Displacement is any activity apparently unrelated to the display, such as feeding or preening. The bird performing this activity is in effect saying, 'I don't know what you're getting so excited about. Don't mind me. There's nothing to worry about. I'm just preening.' It is a behaviour pattern that can be seen in human beings. The small child who has been naughty does it and so perhaps, in a more sophisticated way, does the politician who nervously smooths his hair or adjusts his tie when being grilled by a TV interviewer.

Pair formation

Eight out of ten robins pair up in the males' winter territory. While advertising his territory the male sings from a concealed perch, but betwen late December and March his behaviour may change: he moves towards the centre of the territory, singing more often and from more conspicuous perches.

A female, attracted by this behaviour, approaches him making the high-pitched 'tzeep' contact-call. Early in the season the male may respond aggressively to her approach, but if pairing is to take place he may move towards her singing and making a soft contact-call. As she comes nearer he may peck at the ground and retreat from her. As she follows him this can look like a territorial dispute, but he is actually drawing her into his territory. The female may stop and begin to feed, in which case the male will probably join her. She may leave the territory and he may follow her, but he will not leave for long and will be back within a few minutes. Such displays usually last only a couple of hours, but in one exceptional case continued for five days.

Female birds are attracted by bright colours, so male displays emphasise these. Both sexes of goldfinch have brightly coloured plumage and emphasise their crimson cheeks and bright yellow wing-flashes by crouching on a perch and pivoting on their legs. They lower their wings to show more of the yellow wing-bars and puff their cheeks to expand the bright red flashes, calling with an excited 'tuleep' or 'tu-wee-oo'. As they get more excited their movements grow more exaggerated.

Courtship display

When a female first enters a territory held by a male she will probably be greeted with an aggression display. The female will respond submissively, but will not leave the territory. The male's display then turns from aggression to courtship. The great tit begins to display in late winter, when the flocks break up and males lay claim to breeding territories. The male emphasises his white cheeks and black belly stripe by standing upright and swaying from side to side so that the cheeks are exposed alternately. The reaction of another male would be to either square up to the territory-holder or to fly off, but a female responds submissively.

To advertise his presence the male collared dove gives a repeated cooing call for up to two hours after sunrise in spring. He sits with bill lowered, throat inflated and feathers ruffled, his legs bending with each call. This may be followed by a display-flight, in which the bird rises steeply, sometimes clapping his wings together to make a loud noise.

The female, attracted by the male's calling, lands near him and approaches in an upright position with lowered bill and ruffled feathers. The male bows to her with a display alternating between an upright and crouched position. The neck feathers are ruffled and the air sacs in his neck are inflated. With tail depressed he bows forward until the bill is very low. Then, still swollen, he rises to upright position. He may perform up to five of these bows in half a minute. Throughout the ceremony he raises first one foot, then the other.

Head stretched forward the courting male blackbird (right) approaches his mate with the feathers on his crown and rump raised and his bill open. Once the pair is formed the female becomes more dominant.

The female approaches close enough to the male to preen his neck while he crouches.

Courtship between birds can be drawn out over several days or weeks during which the reproductive cycles of the two individuals are stimulated and become synchronised. Research has shown that the hormone levels of turtle doves are affected by the closeness of a bird of the opposite sex. Those species and individual birds which begin their courtship early in the year tend to spend longer than those that start later.

The length of the courtship also enables the birds to get to know each other, which means each can assess the other's potential as a parent for its offspring. Since there are usually more males than females, it is usually the female that makes the choice of mate. It is important for her to find a mate that will both father healthy offspring and be successful at finding food for her and her family.

The male attributes which attract female attention vary between species and it is scarcely easier to identify the causes of attraction in birds than it is to decide what attracts human females to human males. In many bird species it is the most brightly coloured males which prove the most attractive to females. This attraction must have reasons beyond aesthetics, and it has been suggested it might be

To advertise his possession of a nest-site and his availability as a mate, the male house sparrow approaches a female with gaping bill and puffed chest, turning his body to show her his wing-bars. House sparrows usually pair for life.

Among those blackbirds which stay in the same area throughout the winter and remain to breed in the following summer, the pair-bond often persists from season to season, but a male and female spending the winter together may split up in the spring and seek different mates.

Pair-bonds

For some garden birds the bond between the pair lasts no longer than the breeding season. For others it lasts from season to season until the death of one of the birds.

To reassure its partner, a male wood pigeon gives a low nest-call that is softer than its 'coo-COO-coo-coo-coo' song at intervals for any time up to four hours.

Another bonding ritual is allopreening (mutual preening). Each bird preens the plumage around the head and neck of the other. As well as cementing the bond between the birds, this process may also help to to preen parts which are difficult for the indivual to reach itself.

because brilliant plumage could be evidence of the individual male's resistance to parasites or disease. A female that chooses such an individual may be ensuring that she will have offspring carrying the genes to resist infection.

Among swallows it seems that tail-feather length is the key to a female's heart. At first glance there is little difference between the plumage of males and females, but if you see two birds together the male's tail can be seen to be several millimetres longer than that of the female. Experiments by biologists in which the male's two outer tail-feathers were artificially lengthened showed that these longer-tailed males paired more quickly than those with their tails left at their natural length.

Long tail-feathers may be a sign of the physical fitness of the individual and the female has a vested interest in finding a fit male in order to produce fit offspring with the consequence of maximising the chances of her genes surviving.

Collared doves display to each other on a roof top.

Courtship feeding

Once a pair has been formed, males will often feed their mates. When the female greenfinch wants to be fed she crouches with wings fluttering and bill open and makes faint begging calls. Her mate stands upright and pushes seeds into her bill with his tongue. During the few seconds that courtship feeding lasts three or four beakfuls of food are passed from the male. The female's behaviour, which is a reversion to the begging behaviour of a juvenile, gives the female a chance to assess the food-finding ability of her mate. Finding food is an important feature in species where the male helps to feed the young or where he feeds the female while she is incubating.

There is also a practical effect of courtship feeding as it provides extra food at the time when she is building herself up to lay her eggs.

Pair-bonds

For many garden birds the pair-bond lasts no longer than the breeding season. The birds may separate after the breeding season as they move away from the breeding territory. Some pairs do continue from year to year, however. Those blackbirds which stay in the same area throughout the winter and remain to breed in the following summer may stay as a pair every season until they are parted by death. However, sometimes when a male and female spend the winter together they may split up in the spring and seek different mates. Incompatibility is not only found among humans.

The bond between great tits lasts throughout the breeding season and, although they may re-form for a period during the autumn, they break up in winter. Nevertheless, when pairs re-form in January about three-quarters of those that have survived the winter repeat the pairing of the previous summer.

However, the numbers that survive from one year to the next is as low as 25%. The frequency of re-pairing may be more due to the birds' faithfulness to their nest-sites than to each other. Because they stay in the same area they may come together by coincidence.

Nevertheless just as human beings have practical reasons for maintaining long-standing pair-bonds, so do birds. Each member of the pair becomes accustomed to the other, which helps them to work well together to maintain a breeding territory, to nest and to rear their young. Among long-lived birds, such as seabirds and birds of prey, new, younger pairs often rear fewer young than those which have been together for several seasons. When one partner dies and the other takes a new one the new pair is likely to be less successful in terms of of young reared than the old pair would have been.

Just as human relationship can break down when partners ignore each other, birds similarly must reassure their mates by their behaviour. To maintain the bond between them they perform certain rituals.

It is this behaviour which has given doves the reputation of amorousness and gives rise to the expression 'billing and cooing'.

Billing and cooing

One of the commonest doves is the wood pigeon. Once the pigeons have paired the male begins to produce a low call that is softer than its 'coo-COO-coo-coo-coo' song and given at intervals over periods of up to four hours. This may be followed by one of the pair, more often the female, gently caressing the feathers around the other bird's bill and eye with her bill. This leads to mutual preening, or allopreening, in which each bird preens the plumage around the head and neck of the other. This is presumably the origin of the expression 'billing and cooing' and, as well as helping to cement the pair-bond, it may also help them to preen difficult-to-reach parts.

Nesting

Although some birds lay their eggs on scrapes in the sand or convenient depressions on cliff-ledges, garden birds all build rather more complex nests in which they can lay their eggs and rear their young. Each species chooses sites which are suitable for its own particular nests. Two principles are required – safety from predators, because eggs and nestlings are particularly vulnerable, and protection from the weather, because all extremes of weather in temperate zones can be harmful to birds.

Buildings provide nest-sites for a number of species of birds including the black redstart, which breeds in much of mainland Europe and at some sites scattered across England. It favours large buildings with high song posts and plenty of cavities in which to rest. The natural nest-sites of black redstarts are rocky slopes and cliff-faces.

Long-tailed tits nest in thorny bushes.

Choosing a nest-site

Choice of nest-site is usually the prerogative of the female. However, the males of some species will show females suitable nest-sites as part of their courtship and some may even build several nests from which their mate can make a choice. The male in possession of a territory in which there are very good nest-sites will be attractive to females.

Selection of nest-sites is often a very practical process with prospecting birds balancing twigs in possible places. The older, more experienced birds are less likely to put twigs in places where they fall off the branch, but there is a large element of innate ability in birds to build nests. Birds which hatched the previous summer have never seen another bird build a nest, but they have to find a suitable site, suitable material with which to build the nest and then perform the complex task of building.

Tits prospect for suitable nest-sites as a pair. They may do this several weeks before the breeding season and the female will use the chosen nest-hole as a roost. This is time well spent because it increases her knowledge of the surrounding area, as she becomes attuned to the sounds and the comings and goings. When the prospecting male finds a site he may attract his mate to it by performing a fluttering display-flight, known as the 'butterfly-flight'. He may encourage her to enter the hole by going in himself and calling to her. She may reject several sites until she finds one which suits her.

Long-tailed tits build very complex nests and the prospecting male may suggest suitable sites by building in them. The female may show she has accepted the site by joining him in the building, but if she does not do this, he searches for other sites.

Leave well alone

Looking for nests during the breeding season is a bad idea, because it may disturb the birds at a crucial point in their breeding cycle or attract the attention of predators such as magpies and cats.

The male wren builds about half a dozen nests (taking between one and four days to complete just one of the domed nests) which he shows to his mate inviting her to make a choice. When she has chosen one, she lines it with feathers and hair.

Sometimes birds will build more than one nest because the male is confused, rather than to offer his mate a choice. This confusion usually occurs where there are several suitable sites in very similar places. It can happen in buildings where a bird can become dis-orientated by several sites that all seem the same and will start to build nests in each. At a power station where there appeared to be only one pair of mistle thrushes five nests were found at the same height but 7 m apart among identical iron and concrete pillars.

Sometimes she will make her choice before he has finished and may even join in with the building.

Unnatural nest-sites

Sometimes birds choose nest-sites in places which may seem strange to us, but which are quite sensible to them, because although man-made, they have all the characteristics of natural nest-sites. Some species seem to choose buildings in preference to natural sites. Most house martins choose the eaves of houses, but may be found nesting in a more natural place on the cliffs at Flamborough Head in Yorkshire. The confiding robin seems adept at finding strange places such as telephone boxes. Great tits have been found nesting in pillar boxes and readily take to nestboxes in gardens.

Garden sheds provide nest-sites for robins.

Siting nests

Some owners of very large country gardens may have pheasants nesting in them, but generally garden birds do not nest on the ground. Most garden birds look for a nest-site in trees, bushes or buildings. Quite uncon-sciously gardeners provide many different sites in which they can nest. A large, mature garden is more likely to attract breeding birds than a new one, but even if there are not mature trees and shrubs, there is plenty that can be done to attract nesting birds. Nestboxes can be put up and there are quick-growing shrubs and trees which will provide nest-sites within a short period of time.

Although some gardeners are very snooty about *Cupressus leylandii*, its thick foliage provides nesting cover for greenfinches, house sparrows and even for the flimsy platform nest of the relatively large collared dove.

Garden nest-sites

A swallow's nest on a ledge in a garage.

House martins build mud nests under the eaves.

A song thrush nests among the clutter in a garden shed.

Collared doves build flimsy platform nests in the branches of conifers.

Nuthatches nest in holes in mature oaks.

A lamp provides spotted flycatchers with a nest-site.

Pied wagtails nest between flowerpots in greenhouse.

Ivy, as well as being a source of food for birds, creates places among its branches where birds can build nests. The cup-nests of song thrushes, blackbirds, robins and spotted flycatchers all need nooks and crannies to support them and the dome-nest of the wren may be hidden among the leaves supported by the branches.

Sheds and greenhouses may also provide suitable places to nest. In spring an open window in a garden shed is an invitation to birds that are searching for a place to build. A high shelf near the roof may be a suitable spot for the mud-nest of a swallow, which may also choose to make its nest in a coiled hose hanging on the wall. Blackbirds, song thrushes and robins will all nest among the clutter on the shelves. If birds do pay you the compliment of nesting in your shed, please make sure that there are no traps for unwary fledglings making their first trip from the nest: open tins of creosote or even glass jars can be deadly to them.

Robins take advantage of human activity whenever possible and will build in the space between flower pots in the greenhouse, a place which may also be used by pied wagtails for their nests. Be careful how you water the plants. Hanging baskets provide nest-sites that are safe from cats. Because they are often planted out late in the spring, they attract spotted flycatchers, which arrive to nest well into May.

Several species of garden birds may nest on or in houses. House martins build mud nests under the eaves, but these are sometimes taken over by squatting house sparrows before completion. Sparrows and starlings may enter the house through holes in the eaves and nest in the warmth of the loft. A window in a garage or shed regularly left open may encourage a swallow to enter in search of a nest-site.

The dangers of open nest-sites

Birds whose nests are open cups are vulnerable to predators. Once a jay or a cat has discovered the nest, it has no difficulty in removing eggs or young. The answers for the nesting bird are cover, camouflage and quietness. Hole-nests are vulnerable to fewer predators, but weasels are small enough to enter the holes and agile enough to manoeuvre within the nestbox, while a great spotted woodpecker may chip away at the edge of the hole until it is large enough to allow it to delve into the nest.

Building nests

When human beings make things, their hands are the main part of the body used. Birds have no such sensitive instruments as hands, but nevertheless they build nests which are complex structures of fine materials, which would test even the most dextrous human hands. And they build them using their whole body.

In many cases the nest only needs to be a temporary structure, because it is only used for a period of a few weeks. Once the young have left the nest, it is often abandoned, although it may be used for subsequent broods during the season. Carrion crows build nests substantial enough to last until the next season and, although the crows are unlikely to use it again, it may be used by other species such as kestrels. The nest starts as a platform which the birds turns into a cup by pressing downwards. It turns it body to make the cup circular rather than oblong. As the cup forms the bird brings in material to line it. There may be several layers of lining.

Closely related species often build similar nests. For example, both the song thrush and the blackbird create a structure of twigs, grasses, leaves and mosses strengthened by a cup of mud. While the blackbird lines hers with fine grasses, the song thrush makes hers smooth with a lining of rotten wood or dung moistened with saliva. In very dry summers the song thrush may forego this lining and use fine grasses. Thrushes will often use litter as nest materials and paper, plastic, string and baler twine have all been found in their nests.

The time taken to build nests varies. For the birds which nest early in the season the business of nest-building is often leisurely and they can afford to delay the process if the weather turns bad. An early song thrush may take over three weeks to complete a nest early in the season. Such slow progress may be a result of the bird's slowly increasing hormone levels early in the season. By contrast, later nesters may complete their nests within a few days, because there is an urgency to get breeding underway. Sometimes the late builders do not make such a good job of construction. This may partly be a result of hastiness, but it may also be a sign that these birds are inexperienced because later breeders are often younger birds nesting for the first time.

The tiny goldcrest builds a nest in the twigs at the tip of a branch of a conifer. The nest is usually sited so that it is sheltered from the wind and weather. It is almost spherical and is constructed in three distinct layers. The first is moss, lichens and cobwebs, which are anchored around the twigs. The middle layer is moss and lichens and the inner lining is feathers and hairs. Both sexes may build it, but the male tends to do most of the work and sometimes he is the only nest-builder.

Cup-nests

The nests of song thrushes and blackbirds are classic cup-nests and these are the commonest type of nests among songbirds. However, cup-nests vary in size, shape and materials. The nest of the bullfinch is usually built in thick scrub, which means that few people see it in the breeding season, but it may be found long after use in winter when there are no leaves on the bushes. This nest is made up of a very shallow cup of twigs lined with rootlets.

In contrast, the nest of the chaffinch is very different and much more intricately constructed. It is deep and consists of four layers. The outside is a cup of lichen and gossamer from spiders' webs, lined with a layer of moss and grass, then a layer of grass and a final lining of thin roots and feathers.

Among the largest cup-nests to be built in urban and suburban areas are those of carrion crows, which usually build quite high in trees. The foundation is of sticks and woody stems of plants into which are woven finer twigs, bark and coarse grass. The next lining is moss, grass and lumps of earth and finally there is an inner lining of hair, wool and other fine materials. Sometimes crows will nest on pylons and one pair near London's Heathrow Airport used pieces of wire instead of sticks as the foundation of their nest.

While carrion crows nest in single pairs, rooks nest close to people in villages in colonies. They often do so, choosing mature trees for their rookeries, which means that there may be breeding birds in large gardens. Even though they nest in villages, they prefer to feed in the surrounding farmland rather than gardens. When they are nest-building early in the spring they may be seen flying with large sticks to repair last year's nests.

Wood pigeons build very basic nests in trees. These are flimsy rafts of fine twigs, sometimes lined with

Nest-types

Hole-nest: nuthatches plaster the entrance to their nest with mud to reduce its size to exclude competitors and will even do this when the nest is in a specially built box.

Cup-nest: the chaffinch's nest is deep and consists of four layers – a cup of lichen and gossamer from spiders' webs, lined with a layer of moss and grass, then a layer of grass and a final lining of thin roots and feathers.

Dome-nest: the long-tailed tit's nest is a dome built above a cup, about 10 cm in diameter and 16 cm high. The nest is moss woven together with gossamer and hair, the outside camouflaged with lichen and the inside lined with feathers.

Goldfinches nest from mid-May to early August in Britain. They build their very neat, compact cups of moss, roots and grass and gossamer and seek well-hidden sites in the outermost parts of tree branches.

grasses and leaves built in tree branches or thick hedges. They are only about 20 cm across, which is half the length of the pigeon, so that an adult bird on the nest looks remarkably precarious. However, surprisingly for such flimsy structures, they may be used for successive broods and even in successive seasons.

Dome-nests

Not all birds are content to build cup-nests. Some add a roof. One of the most remarkable and one of the most intricate of all European birds' nests is that of the long-tailed tit. It is not large – about 10 cm in diameter and 16 cm high. Countryfolk variously likened the shape of the nest to old-fashioned bottles, barrels, ovens and puddings, and called these little birds bottle tits, bumbarrels, ovenbirds and poke puddings. In Somerset the birds' skills at nest-building were recognised in the name 'nimble tailor'.

The nest of a long-tailed tit has a dome with an entrance on one side near the top and usually faces south. The basic structure is moss woven together with gossamer and hair. The outside is camouflaged with lichen and the inside is lined with feathers: as many as 2084 have been counted in one nest, but this is exceptional, and the average is 1558. Nevertheless, the nest-building is time-consuming and it takes about three weeks for a pair to find materials and finish the nest.

To accommodate as many as a dozen young a long-tailed tit's nest needs to be elastic. It also needs to be strong, because the parents have to be very active in bringing food to their young and usually make about 2000 entrances and 2000 exits while they are in the nest. From the laying of the eggs to the fledging of the young is five weeks, a period during which the stresses on the structure become increasngly heavy.

Magpies use sticks to construct large nests which they line with a mixture of mud or cowdung and fine roots and sometimes hair and grass. The dome is usually built of thorny sticks. Sometimes magpies build high in mature trees, but they are generally between 2 and 6 m up in large blackthorns or hawthorns. The are often very easy to spot, because of their size and the magpie's habit of beginning to build very early in the year before the leaves begin to appear on the shrubs.

Nests of mud

Several birds use mud as an adhesive in constructing of their nests. House martins and swallows, however, use pellets of mud as building bricks. The house martin nests on buildings in the angle between the underside of the eaves and a wall. The nest is constructed from tiny pellets of mud which are laid like small bricks to make an enclosed cup shape with an oval entrance hole in one corner. The completed nest is lined with down and feathers. The birds collect the wet mud on their bills from river banks or puddles up to 150 m away. Both sexes share the building work, with the male apparently taking the initiative at the beginning. It takes the pair about ten days to build a completely new nest, but old nests may be repaired in a few days depending on their condition.

Although the swallow uses similar materials to the house martin, the working arrangements and the design differ. Both sexes work on the nest but the female does most of the the work and the male, a sort of avian hod-carrier, brings his mate pellets of mud with which to build. The nest is a shallower cup than the house martin's and is built on a beam, rafter or shelf with the top open. The mud is mixed with some plant material and the inner lining is of feathers. Building the main structure takes about eight days and the lining takes another two days.

A house martin brings food to its young. This nest has been built at a traditional site beneath the eaves of a house and is a previous season's nest which has been repaired with new mud. The remains of old nests can be seen to the left of the nest.

Robins choose nest-sites with an open entrance. These may include nest-boxes, discarded saucepans or shelves in sheds.

Nests in holes

Several species build their cup-nests in holes in trees and crevices in rocks and walls. In gardens all the tits (except the long-tailed tit which is not a true tit) nest in holes. Ancient woodland trees of various ages and in various stages of decay have many holes suitable for birds to nest in, but managed woodlands and gardens have few. However, tits will readily use nestboxes designed to mimic natural holes. Research suggests that the number of breeding tits is limited by the number of nest-sites rather than by the amount of food available, because when nestboxes were put up in woodland they were immediately occupied. However, an unoccupied nestbox in a garden may mean that there is not enough food available in the area to sustain a family of birds.

The nest of a great tit is a cup built in a hole. The foundation is mainly made up of moss with some dry grasses and other plants, which the female piles up and after using her body to shape it into a cup, she then lines it with a thick layer of hair, wool and feathers. Because of the confines of the hole there is no need to complete an outer rim round the nest. The time taken is variable and while first nests may take the female great tit between two and 20 days, second nests are usually completed within five days.

Birds are unable to differentiate between fine nylon fishing line and the hair or wool with which they line their nests. However, fishing line or plastic netting introduced into the nest can be deadly, because it can twist round a nesting bird's foot and then snag on a branch, causing the bird to dangle until it dies from starvation or shock.

Nuthatches nest in holes in trees, and they may plaster the entrance with mud to reduce its size, which excludes larger competitors, such as starlings, and predators of the young, such as great spotted woodpeckers. They will also plug cracks with wood chippings and cover them with mud as protection against the weather. The bulk of the plastering is done by the

Siting a nestbox

When you put up nestboxes, do not position them so that they are in full sun or with the entrance facing in the direction of the prevailing wind. Do not put them within reach of cats and it is also a good idea to put them out of human reach to avoid peering into the nest and disturbing the birds.

You can help in providing material for birds nesting in your garden where there may not be enough natural sources by taking human or dog hair from a brush and putting it out for the birds to find.

females, but males will repair the plastering around the entrance hole after the female has started to incubate the eggs. Nuthatches using nestboxes, will sometimes still plaster the front of the box.

Woodpeckers excavate their own nest-holes. A pair of great spotted woodpeckers usually takes between two and four weeks to dig out a nest in a tree trunk 3–5 m from the ground. Although the entrance is only about 6 cm in diameter, it leads downwards to create a nest chamber about 35 cm deep and about 12 cm in diameter. After all the work which has gone into building the nest it is perhaps unsurprising that the nest is re-used in subsequent years. Unused woodpecker nests will be taken over by starlings or jackdaws. Both are hole-nesters and will use nestboxes if they are large enough.

Other users of nests

Nestboxes provide homes for other animals when they are not being occupied by birds. Wasps have been known to build their nests in boxes meant for birds and wood mice are sometimes found in them. Mice will also use nests in hedgerows and sometimes a toad will find a low nest a convenient place in which to hide.

The most numerous non-bird occupants of nests are fleas. These are tiny insects which feed on the blood of their hosts. Most are parasites of mammals and will be familiar to many cat- or dog-owners or to anyone who has ever handled a hedgehog. Some fleas specialise in birds and a few specialise in particular species or groups of species. Their bodies are flattened so that they can pass easily between the feathers and have 'hairs' which help them to stay on their hosts. Fleas are able to jump several centimetres, which enables them to board a new host.

The great spotted woodpecker excavates a nest-hole in a tree trunk in which it will rear a family of between four and seven young.

As larvae the fleas live in their hosts' nests feeding on the detritus from the birds' bodies. The adult fleas wait sometimes for many months for the return of the birds to the nest in spring. There are rarely more than 10 fleas on any individual, even though there may be thousands in the nest. Another blood-sucking parasite of birds is a flat-fly, whose host is a swift. About one in three swifts carry the flat-fly and although there may be as many as 33 on one bird, they do not usually seem to have a permanently damaging effect on the birds.

Courtship and copulation

Courtship leads to copulation, which takes place with greater frequency a day or two before the first egg is laid.

Mating among collared doves is preceded by a display-flight, an intense bowing display and sometimes by aerial pursuit.

A female great spotted woodpecker may solicit copulation by three short bouts of drumming with her bill against a tree-trunk, by fluttering flight or by placing herself sideways along a branch and crouching. The male flaps his wings for balance as he mounts her. During the three-second copulation both birds make clicking and rattling calls.

Copulation among house sparrows is most frequent in the 10 days before egg-laying commences, taking place as many as 40 times a day.

Copulation

Once a nest has been built the female can begin laying her eggs, but in order for the eggs to be fertilised by her mate she must first copulate with him.

The act of mating between two birds is a short and often a hit-and-miss affair. For most of the time birds avoid bodily contact, but, if the male is to pass his sperm to the female, the two birds have to come into close contact. The sperm is passed from the male's cloaca to the female's. The cloaca of each sex is positioned on the underside of the body and the birds have to bring the openings together somehow. Only in species which mate on water, such as ducks, is there a penis which can enter the female's body.

Mating is achieved by the male mounting the back of the female, which twists her tail sideways to allow the contact as he twists his tail in the opposite direction. To achieve satisfactory mating the male must keep his balance and the female must stand firm.

The actual mating takes only a few seconds, but many mating attempts fail. Sometimes this is because of lapses of concentration or the failure of either bird to position itself correctly. Unsuccessful mating may also be caused by a sudden change to aggressive behaviour by one of the partners or the flight of the female.

There is often a prelude to copulation. For example, among collared doves it is often preceded by a display-flight, an intense bowing display and sometimes by aerial pursuit. The female invites copulation by adopting a posture which makes it possible, crouching slightly and moving her wings out of the way by either lifting or dropping them. As the male mounts her, he often makes a nasal-sounding call. Although copulation lasts only a few seconds, it may be repeated very frequently, at intervals as short as three minutes. After copulation the pair sits together, preening themselves. If the female flies off, the male may follow her.

A female may initiate the act. In the case of great spotted woodpeckers she may solicit copulation from her mate by three short bouts of drumming her bill against a tree trunk, by a fluttering flight or by placing herself sideways along a branch and crouching. The male flaps his wings for balance as he mounts her. During the three-second copulation both birds make clicking and rattling calls. When he has finished the male may fly off or both birds may stay on the perch and adopt a sky-pointing posture side by side.

Great spotted woodpeckers copulate about six times a day shortly before and during egg laying, a period of about seven days. During the early part of incubation they continue to copulate two to four times a day.

Eggs

For most bird species there is about a 24-hour gap between the egg being fertilised and its being laid. Encapsulated within the shell is an embryo and a support system that will enable it to develop to the point of hatching. The development usually starts when the last egg of the clutch is laid and the parent begins to incubate, so that all the young hatch simultaneously. However, many birds of prey begin to incubate after the first egg is laid, which means that the young hatch at intervals of one or two days. The eldest of a clutch may therefore be 10 days older than its youngest sibling. The advantage of this is that it increases the chances of survival of the eldest, if food becomes scarce.

The contents of an egg are familiar to anyone who has broken a chicken's egg into a pan. The three main elements are shell, yolk and white.

The shell is a light, but remarkably strong protective covering for the contents of the egg. It consists of three layers – hard cuticle surrounding a chalky central layer which is in turn lined with a membrane. A large number of tiny pores in the eggshell allows gases to be exchanged between the worlds outside and inside the egg. Blood vessels from a second membrane which contains the white (or albumen) enable the embryo to feed. At the blunt end of the egg, between the two membranes, there is a small air space, which is thought to act as a condenser for conserving water.

The albumen is packing for the embryo, protecting it from shock if the egg is moved. It also prevents the embryo from drying out, helps to kill bacteria and provides some nutrition.

Within the protective coverings of the shell and the albumen is the yolk, a fluid rich in fats and proteins, which forms part of the ovum. The rest of the ovum is the small germinal disc, which perches on top of the yolk, and can be seen in a chicken's egg as a white spot, no more than 4 mm in diameter and with a clear centre. From this the embryo grows, sustained by the protein and fat of the yolk. Waste products from the kidneys collect in a capsule of membrane, which can be seen as a patch of uric acid crystals on fragments of broken eggshell.

By the end of the incubation the eggshell will have thinned, because some its calcium will have been used in the formation of the bones of the developing embryo. The reduction in thickness makes it easier for the young bird to chip its way out of the egg, using the horny tip of its bill (known as an egg tooth).

Laying eggs takes considerable energy. The female needs large amounts of food to produce a clutch of healthy eggs. This is one of the reasons for courtship feeding by the male: as well as cementing the pair-bond it helps her to add to her weight without the effort of finding food for herself. The weight of a female blue tit may increase by as much as 50% as she is about to lay: normal winter weight is about 10 g and the weight at laying 15 g, part of which may be the weight of a fully

Blue tits lay clutches of as many as 12 eggs with an interval of a day between each egg.

Cuckoo in the nest

*Only one species in
northern Europe leaves
the rearing of its young
to a completely different
species.*

The male cuckoo's role in family life
is to find females with which to mate,
and the female's is to find the nest
of another species from which she
takes one egg and replaces it with one
of her own. After this she plays no part in
the rearing of her family. She may lay as many
as 25 eggs in this manner, although most probably
will lay fewer than ten.

Individual cuckoos specialise in laying in the nest
of one host species. The most frequent hosts in
north-western Europe are dunnocks (right), meadow
pipits and reed warblers, while in central Europe
garden warblers, pied wagtails and robins are
chosen most often.

The young cuckoo will often hatch before the host's eggs and within 36 hours, although still blind, it will eject the other eggs or young of the host from the nest. The young bird has a dished back to enable it to hold each victim steady as it heaves them one by one over the side of the nest. The foster-parents are busy for the next 18 days or so feeding the young cuckoo until it fills the nest and overlaps its rim. Even when the cuckoo has fledged four to six weeks later, they will have to feed it until it leaves on its migration southwards.

By the time it leaves the nest the young cuckoo dwarfs its foster-parents, which may have to perch on its back to reach its bill.

formed egg – 1.3 g. If she lays 10 eggs over 10 days she will have laid her own weight in eggs. She will need to make eggshells and to do this she collects snail shells and digests them overnight. The calcium from the night's snail shells will go towards the shell of the egg to be laid approximately 36 hours later, because the next day's egg will already have its shell. Most garden birds lay their eggs early in the morning, which saves the female having to carry an almost fully formed egg around all day.

Small birds usually lay roughly at 24-hour intervals, but may stop laying if weather conditions turn and wait for an improvement before completing the clutch. For example, swifts, that normally lay clutches of three eggs at two-day intervals, may increase the interval to up to four days, if changes in the weather mean less food being available.

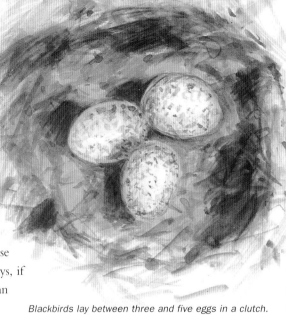

Blackbirds lay between three and five eggs in a clutch.

Ground-nesting waders (which nest only in the most exceptionally located gardens) have eggs whose patterns mimic the shadows cast by the surrounding vegetation. Birds nesting in the branches of trees tend to lay eggs which mimic the dappled effects of the shadows cast by leaves.

Because the young of most garden birds are blind, naked and incapable of walking when they hatch, the eggs do not need to be as large as those which produce young which are covered in down and capable of walking when they hatch (chickens and pheasants belong to this group). One egg of a 17-g great tit weighs a tenth of that of the adult bird. Other birds lay eggs that are proportionally less heavy. Cuckoos weigh about 100 g and lay eggs of 4.5 g, which makes them not much larger than the eggs of the birds whose nests they parasitise.

Eggs of many shapes, colours and sizes

Although we tend to think of all eggs being the same shape as those of chickens', they do come in a variety of shapes. Owls' eggs are almost spherical, whereas swallows lay long, oval eggs. Differences in shape are probably connected with the shape of the birds' pelvis but some shapes clearly have practical advantages over others. Because on many eggs one end is narrower than the other they fit more snugly together in the confined space of a nest.

Birds which nest in holes usually lay white or pale blue eggs, presumably because they have no need of camouflage. This pale colour also has an advantage as it shows up more clearly in the darkness and the parents can avoid trampling on the eggs.

Other birds lay eggs which are cryptically coloured. The ground colour of an egg is set in the chalky part of the shell, but the patterning is in the outer cuticle.

Clutch size

The number of eggs a bird lays in a clutch varies from species to species. Within a species clutch size may also vary. Several theories as to why this should be have been put forward.

Extensive research has been undertaken at Oxford University on populations of blue tits and great tits. Those birds laying later in the season laid fewer eggs, presumably because of diminishing stocks of caterpillars on which to feed the young. Clutch sizes are also smaller when the onset of spring is later and the availability of caterpillars is reduced.

Perhaps for the garden birdwatcher the most interesting factor in different clutch sizes is the differences between different habitats. Blue tits lay slightly more eggs in oakwood (average of 10.9 eggs per clutch) than in other deciduous woodland (average of 9.7 eggs per clutch), but in gardens they lay an average of 8.8 eggs.

The losses of nestlings in gardens are high, many dying because of lack of food. Fifteen days after hatching up to 40% of the garden tits have died and the survivors weigh 3 g less than comparably aged woodland tits. The reason for the difference is that there are plenty of caterpillars for the woodland birds, while the garden birds are struggling to rear their young on greenfly, which take longer to collect as they are more difficult to hold in their bills.

Population may affect clutch sizes. Blue tits and great tits both lay fewer eggs when there is a high density of breeding birds. Younger females also lay slightly fewer eggs than older ones. Another limiting factor is the size of the nest-hole.

The risk of predation may also limit clutch sizes. During the period between laying and the start of incubation the eggs are especially vulnerable to predation and the more eggs that are laid the greater the risk. When a large clutch hatches it becomes vulnerable, because it is noisier than a smaller clutch and there is a greater chance of attracting predators. Producing more young also means the parents must make more visits to the nest, increasing their chances of being ambushed by a predator. The theory that the risk of predation may be the reason for the limit on clutch size may be demonstrated by the greater clutch size of hole-nesters compared with open-nesters: average clutch sizes of hole-nesters appear to be more than a third larger than those of open-nesters.

Number of broods

Many garden birds will rear more than one brood a year. Second broods are not uncommon among blackbirds and song thrushes, which may also attempt a third brood, if conditions are right. The blackbird is likely to attempt a third brood when the summer is wet and earthworms are easy to find in the damp soil. In a hot, dry summer food may be so short that blackbirds may not even rear a second brood.

Some pigeons and doves are multi-brooded. Collared doves nest from March through to November and may rear up to six broods of two eggs. Tawny owls, in contrast, rear only one brood a year, because their responsibilities as parents last so long. Three or four eggs are laid in March at three- or four-day intervals.

The incubation begins with the first egg and lasts about four weeks. It takes another five weeks for the young to reach the stage of flying and then the parents feed them for another 12 weeks.

Incubation

For the embryos within eggs to develop they must be kept warm and development ceases when the temperature falls below 34°C. The parents provide this by transmitting heat from their own bodies. Most incubating birds develop brood-patches, areas on either side of the underside of their bodies from which the feathers are moulted and where the blood-vessels move close to the surface of the skin. The incubating bird settles on the eggs and brings them into contact with the brood-patch. This brings the eggs to body temperature (for most birds about 40°C, rising slightly during incubation) and enables the embryo to develop.

Most garden birds do not begin to incubate until the last egg is laid, but the embryos in the first eggs to be laid survive any chilling. However, once incubation and the development of the embryos begin, they become susceptible to chilling, which is why the incubating bird sits tight for as long as it dares when danger threatens. Camouflage is very important in these circumstances and most song birds have backs that are cryptically coloured so that they are not obvious when sitting on the nest.

Incubating birds with open nests are vulnerable and the incubation period for these species, therefore, tends to be short: as little as 11 days for some goldfinches. Most garden birds in cup nests take about a fortnight, but the hole-nesting coal tit takes up to 18 days and magpies take over three weeks, several days longer than rooks which have more open, and therefore more vulnerable, nests.

It is usually the females who do the incubating, but it is shared in some species, although the bulk is usually still done by the female and it is usually she who incubates through the night. Incubating females are often fed by their mate, which both re-enforces the pair-bond and means that she does not have to leave the nest to find food. Generally the more food the male can bring to her, the more time she stays on the nest and the less time the incubation takes.

Growing up

From hatching to adulthood

For young garden birds the period between hatching and leaving the nest is one of danger. When they hatch their featherless state makes them vulnerable to cold so they must rely on their parents to brood them to keep them warm and dry. As they grow feathers they have less need of brooding, which gives the parents more time to search for food.

Blackbirds are blind, featherless and totally dependent on their parents when they hatch.

Young birds

When adult birds are incubating eggs, they are quiet and unobtrusive. Suddenly, from the moment the first young chicks hatch there is a burst of activity. From this time one begins to see the parents collecting food and flying back towards to the nest with their bills brimming with insects throughout the day.

Song birds are naked, blind and unable to walk when they hatch. They are completely dependent on their parents for food, warmth and protection. However, gamebirds, which are covered in down, are able to walk and to feed themselves within a few hours of hatching.

A mistle thrush feeds its gaping young.

Feeding young

For the parents the next weeks are very busy. Feeding their young takes a large amount of their time. Some, like tits, feed insects directly to their young. They can be seen with bills bulging with caterpillars, a particularly good food for young birds as they are comparatively large and rich in protein. A blue tit which has to rely on greenfly to feed its young takes more time finding the equivalent weight in greenfly, and its offspring do not do so well. It has been calculated that a family of blue tits needs 10,000 caterpillars or 1,000,000 greenflies. Large insects have hard parts which the nestlings cannot cope with, and the great tit will remove the heads from large caterpillars and spiders and the wings from large moths before feeding them to its young.

When the chicks first hatch they need to be brooded to keep them warm. As they develop (initially quite a slow process), the need to be brooded diminishes and both parents can devote most of their time to finding food. The young need more food as they grow and towards the end of the fledging stage, almost all of the parents' time is spent finding food. It takes between two and three weeks for most songbirds to fledge.

All garden birds, even the seed-eaters, feed their young with some animal food, which contains the protein, calcium and moisture required by the growing chicks. Even when they are still blind, chicks will react to the vibration of the parent landing on the side of the nest by opening their mouths very wide. The broad, brightly coloured, gaping mouths and pleading cries of hunger of the chicks stimulate the parents to shove food into them. The parents make no attempt to distribute the food fairly and it is the noisiest, pushiest chick which is given most of the food.

Feathers for blackbirds

The plumage of a blackbird gives clues to its age and sex.

Newly hatched blackbirds are naked and blind.

Within a fortnight they fledge. Both sexes are brown with a vaguely speckled breast and flecked back.

Adult males have shiny black plumages with yellow bills and eye-rings.

In late summer a young male loses most of its juvenile feathers, but retains its tail and most of its wing feathers.

Females are darker than juveniles and have pale throats.

Although the male chaffinch does not help to build the nest or share incubation of the eggs, he does help to feed the young.

Tits carry the food to the nest in their bills and are limited by the number of insects they can hold at one time. During the breeding season bullfinches develop pouches in their mouths either side of the tongue. Into these pouches they cram the spiders, caterpillars, small snails and seeds on which they rear their young. These sacs allow them to make comparatively few journeys to the nest, giving them more time for foraging and reducing the risk of their being spotted by a predator.

The wood pigeon has the ability to eat food and convert it to a 'pigeon's milk', an oily protein- and fat-rich liquid which it regurgitates for its young. The squabs stimulate regurgitation by putting their bills into the parent's mouth. The production of pigeon's milk is one of the factors which enables pigeons to have a much longer breeding season than other birds.

Long-tailed tits may receive help in rearing their young by male siblings of the male parent. These brothers may have failed nests or may have failed to mate. This is not completely selfless, because by helping to rear their brother's progeny the uncles are ensuring the survival of genes that they share with the parents.

Defending the young

Parents of young which are able to walk or run almost from hatching are often very active in the defence of their brood. Waders and ducks are particularly defensive, performing displays intended to distract predators from their young. Songbird parents do not risk themselves and are much more circumspect until the young have left the nest and stand a greater chance of surviving. While they have young in the nest they try not to draw attention to themselves and even avoid flying directly to the nest. When they return with food they fly into nearby cover and approach the nest in a series of short journeys.

Keeping the nest safe

The obvious effect of all the feeding of the young birds is that they defecate. The build up of droppings in the nest could become enormous and there would be a danger of disease and the young birds' plumage becoming encrusted. Songbirds have a system of nest sanitation; the faeces are produced by the nestling in a gelatinous sac and the chick positions itself so that the dropping rests on the side of the nest. When the parent comes with food it collects the sac and deposits it away from the nest. If it were to drop immediately outside the nest the build-up of faecal sacs might alert the curiosity of predators. Similarly the remains of eggshells are removed from the vicinity of the nest as soon as the young hatch.

A rapidly growing nestling is a good source of food for predatory mammals and birds. Weasels are fond of nestlings and are good climbers. Once they have discovered a nest they will make successive journeys to take each of the nestlings. The most active predator on garden birds is a pet cat obeying an instinct to hunt despite its pampered, well-fed life.

Magpies and jays both take nestlings, but each runs the risk of being attacked by the parents. It is quite hazardous for a jay to be attacked by an angry mistle thrush defending its young, because the thrush is not much smaller than the predator.

The greater vulnerability of nestlings in open nests means that the fledging period tends to be shorter, selection having favoured the birds which fledged fastest. Spotted flycatchers have short incubation and fledging periods. They arrive in northern Europe in May and

Keeping your windows clean

House martins do not have the need for concealment, because their nests are usually safe from predators. Their droppings are therefore allowed to drop from the nest. This can be very annoying if it smears the wall or window. To catch the droppings fix a 20-cm square plywood shelf at least 50 cm below the nest.

nest so that hatching coincides with the peak of flying insects around midsummer. Incubation lasts 12–13 days and within another 12 days the young fledge and fly the nest. By comparison, the hole-nesting blue tit has a 14-day incubation after which the young take 16–22 days to fledge. The nuthatch, with a fortnight's incubation, takes even longer to fledge – up to 25 days.

The vulnerability of the nest seems to be a greater factor than size in determining how long the young stay in the nest. One of the larger songbirds, the mistle thrush, with 14 days incubation and a further 14 days before fledging, spends less time in the egg and the nest than the blue tit.

Out of the nest

The work of the parents is not complete once the young have left the nest. The young songbird may have acquired its flight feathers and its muscles may have developed sufficiently for it to fly, but throughout its life it has had its food brought to it. If it were left to its own devices when it left the nest it would survive for only a very short time. The young of most songbirds have to be fed by their parents for two or three weeks after they have left the nest.

Moving away

The young normally leave the nest in the early morning, the parents hustling them away from its vicinity. Moving away quickly from the nest is a precaution against a cat or other predator waiting for the young to make their first foray into the world beyond the nest. This habit means that the human providers of nest-boxes may be disappointed that they do not see the fruits of their generosity, unless they happen to be up early. Some young birds do not find the prospect of leaving the security of the nest especially enticing and they need encouragement from a parent. Reluctant young are lured from the nest with morsels of food offered outside, or sometimes they are pushed from the nest by the frustrated parent, faced with the problem of having to feed young in and out of the nest.

It is relatively easy to see house martins departing from a nest beneath the eaves of a house. Between 15 and 24 days after hatching the parents begin to lure the

A recently fledged goldfinch has black tail feathers and yellow-and-black wing feathers similar to those of the adult, but it lacks the bright red, white and black face markings and its feathers have a wispy, downy appearance.

young from the nest. One parent, usually the female, flies slowly past the nest calling constantly. She may hover outside or even land on the nest, but no food is offered. When the parent lands at the nest the young poke their heads out. Once she has their attention she flies off slowly and deliberately with her wings whirring, and the young usually follow after half a minute or so. After the first flight the young return to the nest and will use it for roosting for a few nights. The ability to fly is instinctive. Once a bird has the necessary flight feathers and muscles, the adult house martins will entice their young to leave the comfort and security of their nests.

Keeping quiet

Once out of the nest young songbirds must maintain contact with their parents, but they must also avoid drawing attention to themselves in case there are predators about. With a nest of their own young to feed sparrowhawks will be watching for easy prey, such

Division of labour

Two species whose young hatch covered in down and which are soon capable of walking are pheasants and moorhens, and they may be found in some larger gardens. The female pheasant incubates up to 15 eggs and the young stay with her for nine or ten weeks. At night she broods the young while they are small and, although they are capable of feeding themselves, she shows them food.

For moorhens there is equality between the sexes in looking after their young. The parents share in incubating the eggs and looking after the young when they leave the nest. The family may split in two with two chicks being looked after by each parent. The family life of the moorhen also involves the young of the first brood helping in the rearing of the second.

as young, inexperienced songbirds. Constant plaintive begging calls will attract the hawk's attention. Therefore, the parents must be watchful for the presence of predators and when one of them gives an alarm call the young immediately go silent.

When they first leave the nest the young birds will stay in deep cover. Blackbirds, for example, will perch comparatively high above the ground for about week. When they do venture to the ground they will have to begin to find their own food, but at about 10 days out of the nest they will begin to flick over leaves in search of food, even though they will continue to be fed by their parents for another 10 days or more. They disappear suddenly from the territory, dispersing farther afield, although it is thought that siblings may stay together during the winter.

It takes young song thrushes three weeks to achieve independence once they have left the nest. Although this species is secretive at this stage, the parents will attack cats which prowl in the region of the young. The larger mistle thrushes feed their young for about two weeks after they have left the nest and from late July onwards the young birds form small flocks and move in a generally south-westerly direction.

A young starling not long out of the nest begs its parents plaintively for food, fluttering its wings, calling and opening its bill.

Learning to feed independently

A parent with a bill full of food will be pestered by the cries of its fledgling which will gape plaintively and quiver its wings. Sometimes the sight of a gaping bill will stimulate the parent to feed the young of another species. If you see a thrush feeding a young starling on your lawn, you are witnessing not an instance of one species helping another, but a mistake born of instinct.

Parents, however, must have a mechanism for releasing the young from their dependence. They need to be able to persuade the young to learn how to feed themselves and they must also persuade them to move away in time to set up their own territories for the next breeding season. For many garden birds there are sound reasons for reducing the dependence of the first brood quickly, in order to have enough time to produce a second brood.

After some days of feeding on demand, the parents start to become meaner and respond only when they are pressed by the fledgling. During the period of

The young starling is successful in attracting the attention of its parent and receiving food, but the parent will gradually withhold food to encourage the youngster to feed itself.

dependence, the young birds prod and examine small objects on the ground. This is the way in which they discover by trial and error what is edible.

Aerial insect-eaters need a high degree of bill-eye co-ordination and it is necessary that the young connect food with flying. Having left the nest 12 days after hatching, spotted flycatchers spend the next week hidden in trees and being fed by their parents. During the second week they become more active, following the parents away from the nest area and becoming more strident in their demands for food, but after a few days the parents become meaner with the food, only feeding the young if asked. They then switch to feeding the young only if they fly to their parents and then begin to reduce the number of rewarded flights. A fortnight out of the nest, the young may find feeding themselves to be a more effective use of their time than begging.

Feeding and flying

Making the connection between feeding and flying is important for young swallows. Fledglings are fed by the parents in flight, but this does not last very long and the parents stop feeding after about five days and within a day or two the young bird is successfully feeding itself.

Tawny owls need parental support for longer than most birds in the garden. After a four-week incubation the first of three or four eggs hatch. The young remain in the nest for about four weeks, although they are not fully fledged until they are about five weeks old. However, it is not until they are about three months old that they become independent. Despite being strong fliers within a fortnight of fledging the young birds make no attempt to hunt for themselves. Failure to find food is the prime cause of death of young tawny owls and over half die in their first year.

Feathers

Among the groups of animals inhabiting the world today only birds have feathers. They provide birds with protection for the skin, insulation from cold, the means of flight and their unique external shape and colouring. Anyone who has seen a chicken plucked and ready for the oven knows that it has a very different shape from the fully-feathered bird that pecks around the farmyard.

Across the surface of the plucked chicken's skin can be seen small raised bumps, 'goose-pimples'. It was from these follicles that the bird's feathers grew. The feather grows from the base and is furled within a sheath. When growth is completed the sheath falls away and the feather, which is now composed entirely of dead material, unfurls.

Attached to the wall of the follicles are networks of muscles which enable the bird to move its feathers. The feathers are manoeuvrable to allow preening, cooling and drying, and the movement that is needed for display.

Feathers perform their functions very efficiently, but they account for no more than 7% of a songbird's total weight. For the plumage to achieve these functions so effectively and weigh so little requires a complex structure involving different types of feathers.

The feathers closest to the skin are the down. These are soft and fluffy, providing the warmth next to the skin, creating a bird's answer to the thermal vest. In young songbirds they are the first feathers to appear within a few days of the naked nstlings hatching.

What might be described as typical feathers are the contour feathers, which consist of a horny quill on either side of which are rows of barbs linked together with tiny hooks known as barbules. Short contour feathers with more or less symmetrical vanes cover the body and grow from tracts across the body. Flight feathers are long contour feathers. The vane on the edge tends to be narrower than that on the trailing edge and flight feathers are stiffer and usually longer than other feathers.

Between the down and contour feathers are two other types of feathers: semiplumes and filoplumes. Semiplumes, which have stiffer quills than down but

soft vanes, are insulators. The hair-like filoplumes always occur next to contour feathers and with nerves at their tips act as sensors which help to keep the contour feathers in place. Bristles are very specialised, spiny feathers which act as guards around eyes or as extra sensors around the bill help insect-eating birds to catch their prey. In some birds they may develop into adornments used in mating displays.

The larger the bird the more feathers it is likely to have. The tiny ruby-throated hummingbird, a garden bird in the United States, has fewer than a thousand feathers while the a swan may have over 25,000. Songbirds have between 1500 and 3000 feathers.

Changing feathers

Feathers are lightweight, complex structures that are subjected to heavy wear. However carefully they are looked after (and birds do take great care of their plumage), feathers have a limited life and are discarded and replaced through moulting. Because feathers take some time to develop, the moult in garden birds tends to be gradual. For small songbirds the process takes about five weeks, for starlings about three months and for carrion crows four months.

A blackbird is a good example to use of a bird which moults from one plumage to another because its young are relatively easily identified. As we have seen, the young are naked when they emerge from the egg. First they develop a buff-coloured down and then after about a week they begin to develop their juvenile plumage. The feathers on the back and upper parts are very dark brown, while those on the breast and underside are reddish brown and buff giving a mottled appearance, which provides camouflage.

When the young blackbirds first leave the nest the primaries and tail feathers are not fully developed and the birds stay in cover for another week, but when they do come out into the open the males and females can usually be told apart by the differences in their colouring. Although both sexes have mottled, rather thrush-like breasts, the males can usually be recognised by their darker wing and tail feathers.

In late summer young blackbirds moult all their feathers apart from those in the tail and some of the primaries. These young birds still have a duller

Young birds

Most garden birds are dependent on their parents for several weeks.

Pheasants hatch with eyes open and covered in down. They leave the nest within a day. They stay with their mother, who teaches the chicks where to feed.

After three weeks in the nest, young starlings leave, but they are fed by their parents for several days or even weeks.

Young starlings, like the young of almost all of the birds commonly breeding in gardens, hatch from the egg naked, blind and unable to fend for themselves.

plumage than the adults. Faint brown flecks can be seen on the breast of the males, whose plumage is browner than that of adults, while the young females moult into plumage that is a rustier brown and their breasts are sometimes blotchier.

During the period between August and October, as the young blackbirds moult into their first winter plumage, there are some strange-looking specimens on our lawns. This first moult begins with the body plumage, then the wing coverts and finally the head. This means that young males may be seen with very dark bodies and brown heads or even with naked heads. These birds, which look like small vultures, are not suffering from a disease, merely waiting for their brand-new feathers to appear. If you see what looks like a strangely coloured thrush-like bird on your lawn in autumn, you can be sure that it is a blackbird if it cocks its tail after it lands.

The blackness of young male blackbirds may vary, but they can be separated from adult males by their dark bills and lack of eye-rings. The bright yellow bill and eye-rings of the adult male do not develop until the middle of the bird's first winter.

Moulting is an energy-consuming business. Energy is needed to renew the feathers and the loss of feathers can reduce insulation, which means that the bird needs to eat more to keep warm. Young birds are particularly at risk during the first moult, because they are unable to find food so well as experienced adults. They are most vulnerable if their first moult coincides with the end of a long, hot summer, because the sun dries the ground and the worms which form the bulk of the blackbird's diet disappear beneath the soil, out of reach of probing bills.

In their second summer the young blackbirds, if they have survived that long, begin their first complete moult. It starts a fortnight after the end of the breeding season and ends with the emergence of new primaries nine to 13 weeks later.

Moult is often very obvious on larger birds. In late summer birds of prey and crows can be seen with ragged wings, where old feathers have been moulted and new ones have not yet appeared.

Colour changes in a bird's plumage may not always be a result of moult. Among finches and sparrows it happens through wear. For example, the black bib of a house sparrow in spring does not appear after a moult. The new feathers that it acquires in autumn have soft tips that are grey-brown, but by the spring these have worn away and the black can be seen, giving the male sparrow a bright black bib.

The last adult feathers a starling acquires are those on the head, giving a partially moulted bird a strange appearance.

A totally white blackbird is affected by a plumage abnormality where it has no pigment. This makes it vulnerable to predators.

Odd plumages

It is very difficult to pick out individual birds of the same species unless they are colour-ringed or have some very noticeable physical difference, such as a damaged leg or abnormal plumage.

The most frequently noticed plumage abnormality is albinism, which is the absence of pigment and shows as white feathers in birds that normally have coloured plumage. Among garden birds this is seen most often among blackbirds, house sparrows, jackdaws and carrion crows. Totally white birds, which may even have red eyes due to lack of pigmentation, are rare.

Other forms of abnormality include: melanism, where an excess of dark pigment makes a bird appear darker than it should be; erythrism in which it appears redder; and flavism in which it appears more yellow. If all the pigments are reduced, the bird's plumage appears to be paler, a condition known as leucism.

These abnormalities are often genetic, and albinistic blackbirds may be recorded in the same area from year to year. Diet can affect the pigments of plumages and the amount of white on albinistic birds appears to increase with age.

A bird with large patches of white on it is ill-equipped to survive in woodlands. As well as the disadvantage of being conspicuous, albinistic birds may also suffer from poor eyesight and deafness, which makes them even more vulnerable.

Feathers

Filoplumes are thin, hairy feathers which may have a sensory function.

Contour feathers give a bird its outline. They consist of two webs on either side of a shaft (or rachis). The webs consist of side branches (or barbs) linked to each other with barbules. The feathers lay on top of each other with the outer web being narrower than the inner web.

Bristles are stiff feathers around the bill which help flycatchers and other insect-eaters to catch their prey.

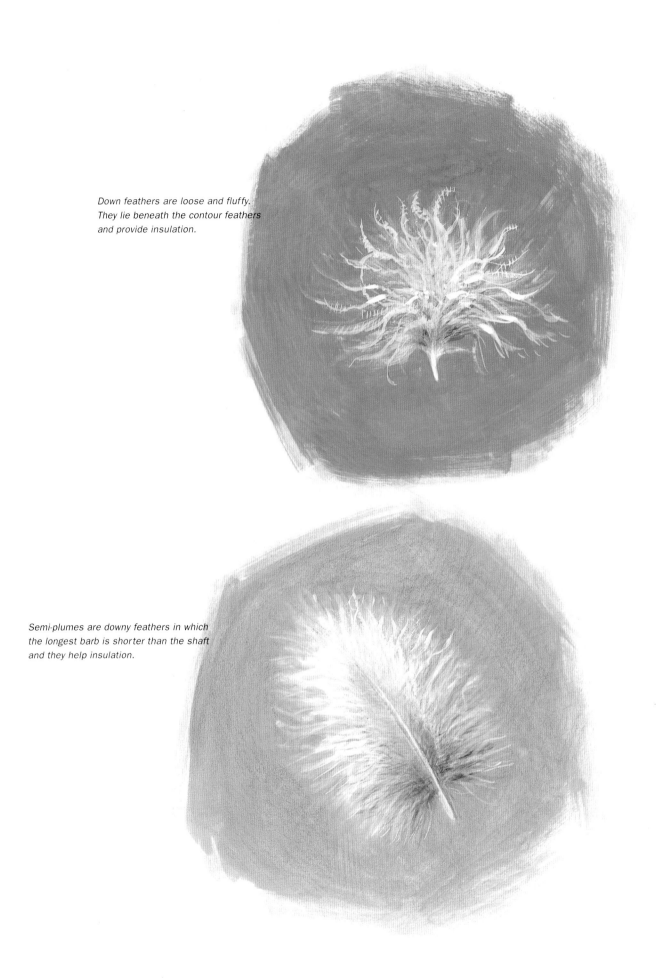

Down feathers are loose and fluffy.
They lie beneath the contour feathers
and provide insulation.

Semi-plumes are downy feathers in which
the longest barb is shorter than the shaft
and they help insulation.

This jay is preening by using its bill to spread oil from the preen gland through the feathers of its back and ensuring that the feathers interlock properly. Birds spend a considerable time taking care of their plumage.

Looking after feathers

The intricate arrangement of feathers, many of which are themselves a complexity of interlocking barbs and barbules, requires care. Birds, therefore, take time each day in making sure that their feathers are in good condition and function effectively.

The most basic and commonly seen feather care is preening, in which the bill is used to rearrange displaced feathers, to clean the plumage and to oil it. Each feather is worked through the bill as if the bird were nibbling it. The oil with which the birds preen comes from a gland on the upper side of the bird near the base of the tail. The preen gland is similar to a nipple and when stimulated produces a fatty oil, which helps to waterproof the feathers. The gland is stimulated by the bill, which the bird also uses to spread the oil over the feathers, transferring the oil on its bill to all the plumage it can reach.

To reach those parts, such as the head, which are beyond the reach of its bill, the bird may scratch with its foot. Alternatively, it may wipe its head on feathers to which oil has just been applied. Scratching is also, as with human beings, a response to an itch. As well as waterproofing, the applied oil may also have antibiotic properties and may be converted by sunlight into vitamin D, which is then absorbed into the bird's skin.

Bathing

This is an activity often seen in gardens with pools or bird-baths and occurs either as part of routine feather care or as a reaction to the plumage having become dirty. When a bird stands on the edge of a pool it is said to be splash-bathing, but it may also enter the water and, standing in the shallows, fluff up its feathers and use its wings to splash water all over its plumage.

House sparrows often use puddles for bathing and may become so drenched that their ability to fly is impaired, making them vulnerable to predators. After the bath they need a quiet, safe place in which to preen their plumage. Swallows take in-flight baths, swooping low over the water and dipping in and out of it as they fly past. Naturally they need fairly large expanses of water for this and usually do it over lakes, large ponds and rivers. Woodpeckers use the rain as a source of bath water and will deliberately spread themselves out in the rain.

Dry puddles and patches of dry soil in flowerbeds give some garden birds a chance to dust-bath. Choosing a dry, sunny spot, house sparrows and wrens, for example, will lower themselves into the soil and using bathing movements will flick the dusty soil over their bodies. Having shaken off the excess dust the bird will then preen itself. The function of dust-bathing may be to remove excess oil or parasites from the feathers, or parasites and broken pieces of feather.

A male house sparrow takes a bath in a puddle and simultaneously spreads its body to take advantage of a shower of rain.

Feather care

A robin preens its feathers by stroking them with its bill to rearrange displaced feathers and to clean any foreign material from them.

Bathing house sparrows dampen their plumage thoroughly, fluffing their feathers to ensure that the water spreads across their bodies.

Spread-eagled on the exposed soil of a flower bed, a song thrush suns itself as part of its feather care.

Spreading oil from its preen gland, a blackbird waterproofs its plumage.

A female house sparrow (above) chooses a sunny spot in a dry flower bed and flicks dust over her feathers, dust-bathing as part of her feather care routine. A jay (below) pauses during its bath in a shallow garden pond.

Spread-eagled on the earth or on a fence, with feathers fluffed and panting, a sun-bathing blackbird may look like a bird in serious trouble, but it is performing part of its feather care routine. This behaviour is usually seen when the sun is at its hottest at mid-day. The sun-bather usually fluffs the feathers on its back and spreads its wings, or in dunnocks and doves one wing is raised vertically with the bird leaning on the ground. The heat of the sun restores and maintains the shape of the flight feathers, but it has other beneficial functions. It may help to spread the preen-oils and to cause them to produce vitamin D. The effect of the sun's rays may also stimulate the activity of fleas and other parasites, making it easier for the bird to pick them off its plumage. Through the fluffed-up feathers rays can reach the skin and may help to keep it in good condition. Finally, it is, course, possible that lying in the sun might be as pleasant a sensation for birds as it is for human beings.

Not every spread-eagled bird is sun-bathing, but may be lying close to an ant colony and allowing them to crawl over its body. Starlings, thrushes and members of the crow family all do this and have been seen to pick ants up and apply them to their plumage. Ants secrete formic acid, which may have a cleansing effect by removing excess oil from the feathers as well as being killing fleas and mites. There may also be some sensual pleasure in this behaviour.

Death and disease

Birds do suffer from diseases, but they are not very obvious and corpses of birds are infrequently found. This is because an ailing bird will be more vulnerable to predators, often being taken before it, literally, falls off its perch and because corpses are eaten very quickly.

Among the conditions that birds can suffer from is salmonellosis, which affects the bird's liver and spleen and can be transmitted through droppings. It can build up at places where flocks of birds feed and drink. Among the garden birds known to have suffered from salmonellosis are greenfinches, which may contaminate each other's food with their droppings. For this reason it is sensible to spread food thinly on your bird-table and to move it from time to time.

A relatively common disease is an avian form of tuberculosis, which was found to be in 4% of wood pigeons in one survey and in over 10% of gulls in another survey. The disease can be passed on to birds of prey which eat birds infected with tuberculosis.

Diseases rarely devastate bird populations, because to do so would be self-destructive. It appears that organisms of disease and parasites evolve to become less harmful to their hosts: an organism which destroyed its host would have less chance of surviving itself.

Garden birds seem to be more likely to die by being taken by a predator or by accident, such as colliding with a window or being hit by a car. It is of course the birds killed by a cat or in a collision which are most obvious to us. However, birds that are taken by predators other than cats, are consumed and their only remains may be pieces of bone in an owl pellet. Injured birds and sick birds creep into cover and, if they are not taken by a predator, will die and be consumed by a carrion-eater, which may be another bird, a mammal or insects. Sexton beetles dig a pit beneath the corpse, cover the carcase with earth and lay in it, so that the decaying bird will provide food for their grubs.

Lack of food also causes death; in cold weather you may come across corpses of birds which were unable to find sufficient food to provide the energy for warmth. There is often little flesh on the breasts of these birds. It could be said that inexperience is the most common reason for death among birds and the first months after fledging are the most dangerous for garden birds. The risk of dying diminishes daily as birds become more experienced, but it remains high throughout their first year of life.

Mortality rates

For bird populations to remain stable a pair need only produce enough surviving young to replace the parents the following year. Since experienced adults have a greater chance of survival than inexperienced young, it follows that numbers of surviving young may not be very large. Indeed, as few as 5% of the eggs laid by small songbirds may survive to become adults. Of the young songbirds which fledge three-quarters will probably die before reaching their first breeding season.

There is high mortality among adult songbirds. Small birds, which breed in the first spring of their lives, lay more eggs and have shorter life-expectancies than larger species, which do not breed until they are several years old and then lay only one egg a year. Thus, blue tits may have an annual adult mortality rate of 70% and a life-expectancy of just under a year compared with a royal albatross's annual mortality rate of 3% and life-expectancy of over 30 years.

Most garden songbirds have an adult mortality rate of between 40 and 50%. Their average life expectancy is a year or so, but some individuals survive much longer. Thanks to ringing studies we know that starlings may reach 20 years old, robins 10 years and house sparrows as many as 12 years.

We all like to think that the birds in our gardens are the same individuals from year to year, and, although this is possible it is more probable that they are different each year.

Coming and going

Movements and populations

The coming of the cuckoo and the swallow in the spring are aspects of bird movements that most of us recognise as examples of bird migration, but there is much more to this topic than the springtime arrival of birds which have spent the winter in Africa. Many species of birds move northwards in spring and southwards in autumn in search of food. This means that in one place there will be different communities of species in winter and in summer.

The movements of birds are caused by variations in the availability of food in different places at different seasons and the need for some birds to leave their breeding areas before weather conditions become too harsh. Birds may move only short distances in search of food from uplands to lowlands, but others may travel thousands of kilometres from one tip of a continent to another.

Ancient myths

The fact of migration has long been recognised. In the Old Testament the prophet Jeremiah wrote, 'The stork in her heaven knoweth her appointed times and the turtle dove and the crane and the swallow observe the time of their coming...'. Aristotle, who died in 323 BC, recorded the times of arrival and departure of migrants in Greece, but he did not have all his facts right. He thought that the redstarts in Greece changed into robins in autumn, when actually both species migrate, the robins arriving from more northerly parts of Europe as the redstarts leave for sub-Saharan Africa. Aristotle also thought that swallows went into hibernation in winter, becoming torpid and spending the winter in the mud at the bottom of ponds, a theory which persisted into the nineteenth century. Some Romans, however, were aware of the homing ability of swallows

and used them to give the results of chariot races. A swallow would be taken from its nest at an out-of-town villa to the Hippodrome in Rome before a race. When the race was over the bird would be released, attached to its leg a coloured ribbon indicating who had won the race, so that the villa's inhabitants knew as soon as possible the result of the race.

Why move?

Where there is a seasonal abundance of food in summer a pair of birds may find it advantageous to run the risks of migrating over a comparatively long distance in order to have the opportunity to rear the greatest number of young. Insects provide high-protein food for breeding birds and many of the summer migrants to Europe are insect-eaters that time their migration and breeding seasons to coincide with the peaks of insect

The familiar call of the male cuckoo is a sign that this summer migrant has returned to Europe from its winter stay in Africa south of the equator. Most cuckoos arrive in northern Europe in April, returning to their breeding grounds a few days either side of the same date each year, and leave on their southern journey in August. The young cuckoo has an innate ability to navigate and migrate southwards on its own.

populations. Swifts and spotted flycatchers, for example, arrive in northern Europe in May and their breeding are cycles timed to coincide with the peak of flying insects on which they feed.

Cuckoos return to their breeding areas with remarkably accurate timing, usually arriving within the same few dates from year to year. Summer migrants to gardens in northern Europe usually return in the same order, chiffchaffs first, followed by swallows, willow warblers, house martins, cuckoos (usually early to mid-April in southern England), swifts and spotted flycatchers.

When to move?

Timing of migration is important. Migrants returning to breed must not arrive before food is available, but must try to do so in time to find the best possible breeding territory. In the most northerly part of Europe it is also important that the birds leave on the journey south before local food runs out. Migrants wait for following winds and good visibility before setting off, but they cannot postpone their departure indefinitely and, if bad conditions

Summer migrants

Spotted flycatchers are insect-eaters which breed in gardens and parks in northern Europe and winter in southern Africa.

Swifts arrive in May, rear one brood of young and leave in July for their wintering grounds south of the Sahara.

Blackcaps which breed in Britain
arrive in April or early May. The
wintering blackcaps which feed
at British bird-tables breed in
continental Europe.

The first house martins usually
arrive in northern Europe in late
March and although most leave
in September and October some
are still here in November.

Siskins (female on the left and male on the right) have spread farther southwards in winter thanks in part to the food put out in gardens. They find peanuts in red nets very attractive.

continue, they eventually have to set off. Delaying spring migration too long would mean missing the period of greatest food supply, while delaying autumn migration would be to run the risk of food shortage.

The stimulus to migrate is genetically programmed. At migration time captive warblers show extreme restlessness and for those species which would normally travel faurthest the period of restlessness lasts longest. These captive birds also begin to build up the reserves of fat that migrant songbirds need to survive migration. Experiments suggest that the stimulus is inherited, but that changes in day-length may also have an effect.

Travelling alone

Although many larger birds, such as cranes and geese, migrate in family parties with the young apparently following their parents, some young birds migrate alone. Young cuckoos, for example, migrate southwards on their own.

Young chaffinches form flocks with females in Scandinavia and migrate in a south-westerly direction, while many males stay in their breeding territories. This was noted in the seventeenth century by the great Swedish scientist Linnaeus, who gave the chaffinch the scientific name *Fringilla coelebs* meaning 'unmarried finch' in Latin. It may be advantageous for the males to stay throughout the winter as they are able to keep good territories and to breed early the next spring. However, against such advantages have to be set the risks of starvation and cold. Inexperienced young males would almost certainly not survive and their movement to the south is, therefore, presumably less risky than staying put.

Those songbirds which breed in Europe and winter in part of Africa south of the Sahara Desert are insect-eaters. They leave before food stocks run out and many supplement their diet with early berries, such as elder and blackberry. Before they begin to migrate they build up fat as fuel for the journey. A small warbler, weighing about 10 g may increase its weight by as much as 70%, before migrating. Fat little migrant songbirds are a good source of food for birds of prey, and migrants crossing the Mediterranean have to run the gauntlet of Eleonora's falcons. These birds nest on cliffs and purposely breed late so that they can feed their young on the large numbers of migrating warblers and other small migrants passing through in late summer.

Watching migration

In some parts of Europe large birds such as geese, cranes, storks or birds of prey can be seen on migration at the right time of year. However, the migration of smaller birds is not usually very obvious. In most gardens we are aware of migration by the arrival of the migrants, often by hearing them – calling cuckoos, singing blackcaps and chiffchaffs. Swallows and martins gathering on telephone wires in September is a sign of migration. The movements of swallows and house martins may be obvious along or beside rivers, or along ridges, especially in autumn. These birds feed in flight and migrate by day, so groups of about a dozen may be seen passing through, feeding on insects as they go. Sometimes in coastal scrubland in autumn there may be a sudden 'fall' of small migrants, when weather conditions suddenly change and interrupt their migration.

Many songbirds migrate at night and it is possible, double-glazing and traffic noise permitting, to hear the 'tseep' contact-calls of redwings as they fly south on autumn nights. Night-time migration reduces the chance of predation by birds of prey; gives the birds the opportunity for daytime feeding; has stars to aid navigation and is cooler, which prevents the birds from suffering the effects of dehydration.

Height, speed and routes

With the wind behind them birds are able to fly high. When it is against them, the birds fly closer to the ground (where friction makes the wind speed slower) and they tend to follow rivers, mountain ranges and coasts. Songbirds usually fly to between 1000 and 2000 m at the start of migration, but they gradually fly higher as the journey progresses. As their fat reserves are used they become vulnerable to dehydration and fly higher where the air is cooler, which guards against dehydration.

A small insect-eating songbird flies between 200 and 250 km in a night at a speed of 30–40 kph. They start at dusk and land in convenient cover shortly before dawn. Thrushes fly a little faster at almost 50 kph and wood pigeons, which cross the North Sea to Britain each autumn, reach 60 kph.

Generally migration across Western Europe tends to be on a north-west to south-west axis with the birds then shifting to a north–south axis to Africa. Some birds fly south-west from eastern Europe and Russia in autumn and then south from the Mediterranean. Migration routes are not fixed permanently and they may change with the climate and as man changes the environment. As recently as 7000 years ago much of Europe was covered by ice, therefore many of the areas where insect-eating songbirds now breed would have been unavailable to them. As the ice retreated new areas were opened up and birds moved in to make the most of the opportunities, moving back again in winter as the areas froze again and so establishing the habit of migration. Farther south, areas of desert in North Africa have increased, which means that migrants crossing the Sahara have farther to fly.

Effects of feeding migrating birds

Feeding garden birds in Britain has affected the migratory behaviour of some birds. Siskins are birds of conifer forests in uplands that move south-westwards in winter. In 1963 they were first recorded feeding at garden bird-tables, and are now regularly seen in gardens in southern England and, helped by commercial afforestation, has become a more common breeding bird in several parts of Britain, including Devon, Dorset and the New Forest.

Another bird encouraged to change its habits by the availability of food in gardens is the blackcap. Over the last 50 years, records of this warbler wintering in Britain have increased. In mainland Europe there are blackcap populations which do not migrate in autumn, but birds from Scandinavia move south-west in autumn, crossing the North Sea and passing south to winter south of the Sahara. However, some blackcaps remain in western Europe throughout the winter. Breeding experiments with blackcaps from the migratory and non-migratory populations show that the impetus to migrate or not to migrate becomes stronger with each generation. Such changes in behaviour are not uncommon and there are places in northern Europe where blackbirds are now resident when a few hundred years ago they migrated south in winter.

Migration of swallows

In September swallows gather on
roofs and telegraph wires before
flying south for the winter.

They cross the Mediterranean
on a broad front in late
September and October.

Swallows will return in April to
their nest-sites of the previous
year, if they survived their
journeys to Africa and back.

In February the swallows begin to gather for the return journey.

By mid-November swallows are numerous in their African wintering grounds, finding insects disturbed by the herds of wildebeest as they had found them disturbed by cattle in Europe.

Crossing the Sahara is particularly hazardous and many individuals do not survive this part of the journey.

Navigation

To make their long journeys small birds have to navigate accurately, a feat which they achieve with great success, as they return to the same breeding sites and wintering areas from year to year. The ability of birds to navigate so accurately is not yet completely understood. Experiments have established that somewhere in the migrant's head is the 'mechanism' for navigation. Also the bird must have some form of 'clock', which is vital if it is to fly in the right direction using the position of the sun. Those that migrate at night must also have a compass mechanism related to the stars and moon.

The ability to recognise landmarks must play some part in the bird's long-distance navigation and clearly is important to its ability to return to the same nest-site after a winter's absence. As well as eyesight, birds use their sense of smell and hearing to find their way.

Irruptions

Not all migrants travel the same distance each year from their breeding grounds to their winter quarters. While the warblers, for example, travel to the same place each year, there are some species whose food supplies cannot be predicted. They travel as far as they need to in search of food and are known as irruptive species.

Many irruptive species are seed-eaters which depend on the seeds of trees, whose crop varies from year to year. In some years there is profusion, in others a dearth. When the seed crop fails there, birds have to keep moving until they find food. Siskins, redpolls and bramblings are all finches which are subject to irruptions.

The nutcracker is a Siberian crow which irrupted in 1968 when the pine crop failed. A few stayed in Belgium and now at least 60 pairs breed there. Perhaps the most beautiful irruptive bird likely to be seen in gardens is the waxwing, which is both good-looking and relatively tame. If one visits your garden, make the most of it, you may not be visited by them again for many winters.

The berries of hawthorn attract a waxwing.

Winter visitors to the garden

Siskins (above, right), which in Britain breed mainly in Scotland and Wales, are becoming common winter visitors to gardens where they feed on peanuts.

Blackcaps on bird-tables in winter are visitors moving westwards from mainland Europe.

In very hard weather fieldfares may be attracted to the garden to feed on windfall apples or pears.

Berry-bearing shrubs will attract redwings to the garden. These are migrants which breed in Scandinavia.

Roosting

Sleeping and keeping warm

Birds, in common with other animals, need to sleep. They do so at night on a convenient perch or, if they are nocturnal, during the day. Depending on the species and the time of year, they may roost singly, in pairs, in family groups or in large flocks.

In winter, cold is the major problem faced by roosting birds at night, and they have developed behaviour patterns which minimise the harm it can do. Although it can be difficult to watch the roosting and sleeping of many birds it is possible to see some of this behaviour in or from the garden. A well-known example of roosting behaviour is shown by the large flocks of starlings which each evening travel several kilometres in tight flocks to the night-time roosts in town and city centres.

Songbirds, like this female chaffinch, which sleep perched on a branch, keep their balance because the tendons in their legs and feet tighten as the bird relaxes.

Pied wagtails usually feed as individuals but return to communal roosts each evening in the winter. The roosts are often in buildings which are especially warm, such as greenhouses, hospitals or power stations.

Sleeping

For about eight hours in every 24 birds sleep. For most birds, but not owls, this is done mainly at night. Many songbirds sleep perched on a narrow branch and in order for them to keep their balance, there is a mechanism by which the tendons in the leg and foot tighten as the bird relaxes, enabling it to maintain its grip.

No one is sure why birds or indeed other animals need to sleep. We all know the feelings of tiredness if we are deprived of sleep and notice that we sleep longer and more deeply after long periods without sleep. Its function may be to stop animals from being active during the periods of the day and night which would make their activities dangerous. In other words, sleep is a safe way for diurnal animals to spend the night and nocturnal ones the day. Other theories are that sleep enables animals to recharge their nervous systems in some way or that inactivity is necessary in order that the information that the bird has received during the day can be processed.

Studying sleep in wild birds is very difficult, because it is not easy to find sleeping birds and when they are found they may be easily disturbed if approached. However, observation in the field and among captive birds has given us some information. Like human beings birds undergo two types of sleep – deep and shallow. In deep sleep the bird is less sensitive to disturbances, but even so it may still blink its eyes. Blinking is a peculiarity of sleeping birds. The rate of blinking is greatest during shallow sleep and may be as frequently as every few seconds. The eye opens and remains open for a few seconds. If there is apparent danger the eye stays open longer. When birds are roosting in flocks they blink less often.

Roosting garden birds

A nocturnal hunter, the tawny owl roosts by day, choosing a high perch in a tree, near the trunk.

A blackbird holding a territory will roost at night in a thick bush, often against a wall.

Roosting dunnocks choose a perch 1–2 m from the ground in a hedge. Often two roost togeer.

At night a moorhen will roost on a branch overhanging water.

Roosting places

Nests are places for rearing families rather than for sleeping, but the parent that is not incubating eggs or brooding young may roost near the nest on a convenient perch. During the breeding season songbirds roost either singly or in pairs. When the pair roosts together the male wakes first and begins his contribution to the dawn chorus and within a few minutes the female wakes and begins to preen.

Woodpeckers and treecreepers perch vertically against the trunks of trees when roosting. Treecreepers choose depressions in the bark and will excavate these in the soft bark of the trunks of mature redwoods in large gardens and parks. The bird flattens itself into a depression and fluffs its feathers. During the day you can tell which of the oval depressions has been used recently by the droppings below it.

Communal roosting

Once out of the nest families may roost together, and outside the breeding season finches, thrushes, starlings and wagtails may roost in flocks. There are advantages to communal roosting because many individuals increase the likelihood of a predator being spotted. Of course, a large flock of birds flying to a roost may itself be more likely to attract the attention of a predator, but this risk may be outweighed by the fact that a greater number of individuals decreases the odds of any one individual being caught. Starlings have the ability to fly in large, tight, swirling flocks which may confuse a predator, and may even use force of numbers to drive it away.

In winter birds are vulnerable to the temperature drops that occur at night and communal roosting helps them to keep warmer than if they roosted by themselves, especially if they are at the centre of the roost.

In very cold winter weather, wrens may roost in nestboxes put up for tits and nuthatches. They may roost communally; on one occasion 61 wrens were recorded in one box.

Long-tailed tits

Two long-tailed tits roosting side by side make a 27% energy saving and the addition of a third bird will increase the total to 39%, giving each bird a greater chance of survival. Roosting long-tailed tits choose a perch deep in thick cover in a thorn bush or on an ivy-clad wall. They perch in line, huddling close and fluffing their feathers against the cold. From their first night out of the nest the young tits roost together. At first each tries to take the central positions, but a hierarchy develops with the top birds taking these and the less dominant birds taking the positions at the end. In cold weather it is the birds at the ends of the row that die first, a clear demonstration of the survival of the fittest. The roosting behaviour of long-tailed tits is vital to their survival in hard conditions and it may even be the main reason for the highly gregarious behaviour of this species outside the breeding season.

Short-toed treecreepers

Short-toed treecreepers roost in groups on sheltered walls in mainland Europe. In one group 20 were recorded entering/leaving a roost. They were positioned with their heads pointing to the centre and their tails pointing outwards, but never more than 14 individuals were seen because some were so deeply buried in their do-it-yourself duvet.

Wrens

Nestboxes, which hve been put up to be used for nesting tits and nuthatches, or disused house martin nests may be taken over by wrens for communal roosting when the weather freezes in winter. One nestbox roost contained 61 birds and 96 birds were found in a roost in a loft. When large numbers of wrens roost together it may take them from 15 to 30 minutes to enter a nestbox, some birds apparently going in and out more than once. Once inside the birds settle themselves into a ball with their heads pointing inwards.

Finches

Finches feed in flocks in winter and roost communally at night, sometimes in mixed flocks. Thus chaffinches, linnets and greenfinches may be found roosting together. They seem to favour evergreen bushes. Up to an hour before dusk they arrive at their roost and perform communal displays, often involving circling it with a hesitant, bounding flight, alighting in the branches of nearby trees and eventually dropping to the roost.

Large communal roosts

In winter, species which range over long distances in search of food often spend the night in large communal roosts. While the whole roosting flock may not feed together, it is composed of smaller feeding flocks. It seems probable that in some way not yet fully understood the roost acts as an information exchange about places which are good sources of food. Pied wagtails travel long distances to join communal roosts and some contain over 1000 birds. One in a reedbed on the River Medway in Kent was actually calculated to have at least 5000 birds. Although pied wagtails roost in natural sites such as trees and bushes, they have learned that buildings can provide them with warmer roosting sites. Greenhouses, supermarkets, hospitals, offices and power stations have all been exploited as roosts by pied wagtails. From autumn through to early spring the wagtails will perform circular flights over the roost in tightly packed flocks. They may do this up to a dozen times in an evening and this behaviour may be a stimulus for migration or perhaps for the dispersal of some members of the flock, to prevent a build-up of too many birds for the food available.

Perhaps the best known and most obvious of communal roosters are starlings, which may roost in flocks of hundreds of thousands in winter. Starling roosts can be seen and heard in city centres, where the temperature is usually higher than in the countryside but the birds move into the suburbs and nearby countryside to feed in smaller flocks during the day. Communal roosts continue to be used during the breeding season by male starlings and unmated birds. Like other communally roosting species starlings perform aerobatic displays before going to roost for the night. However much some people dislike the noisy, apparently greedy behaviour of these birds, their pre-roost flight is one of the great spectacles of bird behaviour. As smaller flocks join the main flock, thousands or even hundreds of thousands of birds wheel in tight, ever-changing formations, like an animated cloud.

Roosting together

On cold nights treecreepers may search out sheltered positions, in which small groups may roost together, with their heads pointing to the centre and their tails pointing outwards.

Families of long-tailed tits roost together side by side at night. The birds in the centre are dominant and keep warmer than those at either end of the row.

The most conspicuous roosting birds are starlings which gather in groups several hours before roosting to perform spectacular pre-roost aerobatics.

Several species of finch may roost together in winter, often in mixed flocks, performing displays in flight, circling the roost with a bounding, rather hesitant flight.

LIST OF BIRD SPECIES MENTIONED IN THE BOOK

Barn owl *Tyto alba*

Black redstart *Phoenicurus ochruros*

Black-headed gull *Larus ridibundus*

Blackbird *Turdus merula*

Blackcap *Sylvia atricapilla*

Blue tit *Parus caeruleus*

Bullfinch *Pyrrhula pyrrhula*

Buzzard *Buteo buteo*

Canary *Serinus canaria*

Carrion crow *Corvus corone*

Chaffinch *Fringilla coelebs*

Chiffchaff *Phylloscopus collybita*

Coal tit *Parus ater*

Collared dove *Streptopelia decaocto*

Common whitethroat *Sylvia communis*

Cuckoo *Cuculus canorus*

Dunnock *Prunella modularis*

Eleonora's falcon *Falco eleonorae*

Feral pigeon *Columba livia*

Fieldfare *Turdus pilaris*

Garden warbler *Sylvia borin*

Goldcrest *Regulus regulus*

Golden eagle *Aquila chrysaetos*

Goldfinch *Carduelis carduelis*

Great spotted woodpecker *Dendrocopos major*

Great tit *Parus major*

Greenfinch *Carduelis chloris*

Green woodpecker *Picus viridis*

Grey heron *Ardea cinerea*

Hawfinch *Coccothraustes coccothraustes*

Hobby *Falco subbuteo*

House martin *Delichon urbica*

House sparrow *Passer domesticus*

Jackdaw *Corvus monedula*

Jay *Garrulus glandarius*

Kestrel *Falco tinnunculus*

Kingfisher *Alcedo atthis*

Lesser whitethroat *Sylvia curruca*

Little owl *Athene noctua*

Long-tailed tit *Aegithalos caudatus*

Magpie *Pica pica*

Marsh tit *Parus palustris*

Meadow pipit *Anthus pratensis*

Mistle thrush *Turdus viscivorus*

Moorhen *Gallinula chloropus*

Nightingale *Luscinia megarhynchos*

Nutcracker *Nucifraga caryocatactes*

Nuthatch *Sitta europaea*

Pheasant *Phasianus colchicus*

Pied flycatcher *Ficedula hypoleuca*

Pied wagtail *Motacilla alba*

Redpoll *Acanthis flammea*

Redstart *Phoenicurus phoenicurus*

Redwing *Turdus iliacus*

Reed warbler *Acrocephalus scirpaceus*

Robin *Erithacus rubecula*

Rook *Corvus frugilegus*

Royal albatross *Diomedea amsterdamensis*

Ruby-throated hummingbird *Archilochus colubris*

Sedge warbler *Acrocephalus schoenobaenus*

Serin *Serinus serinus*

Short-toed treecreeper *Certhia brachydactyla*

Siskin *Carduelis spinus*

Skylark *Alauda arvensis*

Song thrush *Turdus philomelos*

Sparrowhawk *Accipiter nisus*

Spotted flycatcher *Muscicapa striata*

Starling *Sturnus vulgaris*

Swallow *Hirundo rustica*

Swift *Apus apus*

Tawny owl *Strix aluco*

Treecreeper *Certhia familiaris*

Waxwing *Bombycilla garrulus*

White stork *Ciconia ciconia*

Willow tit *Parus montanus*

Willow warbler *Phylloscopus trochilus*

Wood pigeon *Columba palumbus*

Wren *Troglodytes troglodytes*

SELECT BIBLIOGRAPHY

Arnold, E.N. and Burton, J.A., *A Field Guide to Reptiles and Amphibians of Britain and Europe.*, Collins, 1978

Brooke, Michael and Birkhead, Tim, *The Cambridge Encyclopedia of Ornithology,*

Cambridge University Press, 1991

Burton, Robert, *The RSPB Birdfeeder Handbook*, Dorling Kindersley, 1990

Campbell, Bruce and Lack, Elizabeth, *A Dictionary of Birds*, Poyser, 1985

Chinnery, Michael, *Collins Guide to the Insects of Britain and Western Europe*, Collins, 1986

Cramp, Stanley, *The Handbook of Birds of Europe, the Middle East and North Africa,*

Oxford University Press (vols 1–8), 1977–1994

Glue, David, *The Garden Bird Book*, Macmillan/BTO, 1982

Higgins, L.G., and Riley, N.D., *A Field Guide to the Butterflies of Britain and Europe*, Collins, 1970

Imms, A.D., *Insect Natural History*, Collins, 1947

Jonsson, Lars, *Birds of Europe with North Africa and the Middle East*, Helm, 1992

Newton, Ian, *Finches*, Collins, 1972

Perrins, C.M., *British Tits,* Collins, 1979

Simms, Eric, *British Larks, Pipits and Wagtails*, Harper Collins, 1992

Simms, Eric, *British Thrushes,* Collins, 1978

Simms, Eric, *British Warblers*, Collins, 1985

Smith, Malcolm, *The British Amphibians and Reptiles*, Collins, 1973

Soper, Tony, *The Bird Table Book*, David & Charles, 1992

Wingfield Gibbons, David, Reid, James B. and Chapman, Robert A.,

The New Atlas of Breeding Birds in Britain and Ireland: 1988–1991, Poyser, 1993

Wood, Nigel, *Birds in Your Garden*, Hamlyn, 1985

TAKING YOUR INTEREST FURTHER

Organisations to join

There are two organisations that anyone who cares about the future of birds and other wildlife in the United Kingdom should join. The first is the Royal Society for the Protection of Birds, whose growth and increasing effectiveness has been one of the conservation successes of the last few decades.

By becoming a member, you help to support the RSPB's campaign to improve the lot of birds and other wildlife with which the lives of birds are so closely linked. With increasingly centralised government it is important to have a vigorous and effective voluntary organisation whose objective is the better conservation of birds and the places where they live. It is not the RSPB's style to take on a campaign without having the facts to back its claims. Its national and international campaigns are backed by well-researched facts.

Because they have built a network of 132 nature reserves, covering 92,900 ha, RSPB staff have an expertise in managing land for nature conservation, providing the conditions in which wild plants and animals can thrive. Most of these reserves are open to visitors and there is no entry charge to members. Many reserves have observation hides so that the birds can be viewed closely and many have facilities for the disabled.

If you are already a member of the RSPB, you should consider also joining your local Wildlife Trust. The RSPB and the Wildlife Trusts are allies in the fight for nature conservation and many people are members of both. Individual Wildlife Trusts cover counties or groups of counties and there are Urban Wildlife Trusts in some cities. The strength of the Wildlife Trusts lies in their local involvement, but they are also able to act on a nationwide basis in support of national campaigns such as that aimed at the prevention of important wildlife areas being dug up in order to provide peat for use in gardens. Nationally, the Wildlife Trusts own or manage about 2000 nature reserves. These cover 55,000 ha and range from tiny areas such as ponds in which great crested newts breed to large internationally important reserves that are internationally important because of the wildlife they support. There are so many Wildlife Trust reserves that you can seldom be far away from one, which gives Trust members who want to do something practical for wildlife beyond the boundaries of their gardens an opportunity to become involved in the management of a nature reserve near home.

The best way for the newcomer to learn about birds or wildlife generally is to meet other enthusiasts. Both the RSPB and the Wildlife Trusts make this possible through their networks of members' groups. Each group has its own personality and reflects the enthusiasms of its individual members but most have varied programmes which include talks, field outings, conservation work parties and fundraising.

Bird gardening is often a feature of local group activities with the building of bird-tables, nestboxes and bat roosting-boxes and creating nurseries of garden plants for wildlife. Many local groups sell peanuts and seeds to put out for the birds.

If you want to take your birdwatching further and take part in national surveys on birds, you should consider joining the British Trust for Ornithology. This is a voluntary body whose nationwide network of members has added immeasurably to our knowledge of birds for 60 years. Among the BTO's achievements have been mapping the distribution of breeding birds in Britain and Ireland (in conjunction with the Irish Wildbird Conservancy), ringing birds to find out their movements, a garden bird feeding survey and a common birds survey. It is projects such as these which provide evidence on which decisions affecting the conservation of birds can be taken. For example, it was evidence from the BTO which first alerted conservationists in the 1960s to the effect of persistent chemicals in the environment and the BTO then provided the information about the birds whose populations have improved thanks to the use of the chemicals in the UK having stopped.

For the young

Both the RSPB and Wildlife Trusts have branches for young people. The RSPB's Young Ornithologists' Club with its own colour magazine, local group scheme, nationwide surveys and other activities make it a must for young birdwatchers or would-be birdwatchers.

The YOC sometimes runs projects and surveys in co-operation with Wildlife Watch, the Wildlife Trusts' junior branch. Wildlife Watch covers all wildlife and as well as providing information about the natural world it organises projects aimed at providing information which can be used in conservation campaigns.

Books to read

As you become more interested in birds you will want to buy more books about them. The titles mentioned here will help you start to build your own library of bird books.

Identifying birds

First, there is the problem of identifying the birds that visit your garden. The number of books available nowadays is huge and the beginner can be bewildered by the variety of titles and the number of birds they cover. Most of the guides to British birds also cover Europe and may include several hundred species of which only a small proportion will ever feature on most people's garden bird lists.

Unless your garden overlooks a lake, lies beside a river, has a sea view or a similarly unusual outlook, the list of birds seen in or from your garden will not be enormous and you really need a bird book which covers about 100 species. However, there is nothing which is so limited. The nearest are two titles to which the RSPB has put its name – *The RSPB Guide to British Birds* by David Saunders, published by Hamlyn and *The RSPB Book of British Birds* by Peter Holden and JTR Sharrock, published by Macmillan. Each of these covers about 200 of the commonest birds.

The Mitchell Beazley Birdwatcher's Pocket Guide by Peter Hayman is conveniently pocket-sized, but it covers 350 species including several European species that are either very rare or have never been seen in the wild in the UK. Its great advantage lies in its showing the birds from several angles, which is a great help in identification.

Bird gardening

Two books, which cover all aspects of attracting birds to your garden and also help to identify them are Tony Soper's *The Bird Table Book*, published by David & Charles, and *The RSPB Birdfeeder Handbook* by Robert Burton, published by Dorling Kindersley. Each carries an identification section and includes information about feeding birds, including planting flowers and bushes to attract them, and providing nestboxes for them.

The Bird Garden Book, edited by David Glue and published by Macmillan, is based on the results of BTO surveys, has information about the needs of birds in gardens and an excellent chapter on studying birds in the garden.

Information about birds

For basic information about 200 or so species *The Complete Book of British Birds*, published by the AA and RSPB, is a good start. It also gives details of 300 sites at which to see birds in Britain and Ireland.

For a comprehensive reference book about birds, it would be difficult to better *The Cambridge Encyclopedia of Ornithology* edited by Michael Brooke and Tim Birkhead. It tackles biology, behaviour, ecology and conservation.

The books mentioned here would make the basis of a good library of bird books. The possibilities are almost limitless. There are many field guides to the birds of Britain and Europe and the nine-volume *Handbook of Birds of Europe, the Middle East and Africa*, which is also known as *The Birds of the Western Palearctic* (*BWP*) and gives detailed information about the lives of birds.

There are books devoted to single species and others which deal with the problems of birds and the need for their conservation. Once you become even more interested in birds you will find that the number of books you buy will increase.

Useful addresses

Write for details about the RSPB and/or YOC to:
RSPB,
The Lodge,
Sandy,
Bedfordshire
SG19 2DL

For details of your local Wildlife Trust and/or Wildlife Watch to:
The Wildlife Trusts,
The Green,
Witham Park,
Waterside South,
Lincoln LN5 7JR.

For details of BTO membership, write to:
BTO,
The National Centre for Ornithology,
The Nunnery,
Thetford,
Norfolk
IP24 2PU.

INDEX

*References in **bold** are to illustrations*